COMMUNITIES
AND BUILDINGS

GS 1185

COMMUNITIES AND BUILDINGS

Church of England Premises and Other Faiths

A Report prepared for the General Synod
of the Church of England by the Board of Mission's
Inter-Faith Consultative Group

Board of Mission of the
General Synod of the Church of England

ISBN 0 7151 5536 9

GS 1185

Published 1996 for the General Synod Board of Mission of the Church of England by Church House Publishing

© *The Central Board of Finance of the Church of England 1996*

Printed in England by Bourne Press Ltd

Contents

The Inter-Faith Consultative Group 1995

Chairman   The Rt Revd Christopher Mayfield, Bishop of Manchester

Members   Mrs Barbara Butler

Dr Owen Cole

Dr Gavin D'Costa

The Revd Canon David Gillett

Miss Vasantha Gnanadoss

The Revd Canon Dr Roger Hooker

The Revd Canon Michael Ipgrave

The Rt Revd Dr Michael Nazir Ali, Bishop of Rochester

The Revd Alan Race

Dr Elaine Sugden

Representatives Mr Alan Brown (Board of Education)

The Revd Richard Crowson (Board for Social Responsibility)

The Revd Michael Thorpe (Hospital Chaplaincies Council)

Secretary   The Revd Canon Dr Christopher Lamb

Administrative Mrs Pat Cutting
Secretary

Preface

The Church of England is blessed with a wealth of church buildings inherited from another age. In determining our responsibilities towards this heritage and to the needs of the current time, we are compelled to take into account a reality which would have astonished our ancestors – namely, the vigorous communities of other faiths in many of our large cities. These Hindu, Muslim and Sikh communities, no longer migrant but still not fully established in England, often look for help to the Christian churches when they require the use of property temporarily for their meetings, or when they hope to lease or purchase property on a more permanent basis.

The Church of England, like other English churches, has to decide what its policies on these matters should be. We have to look at our own distinctive situation, which is very different and in many ways more privileged than in other parts of the world, where different considerations will rightly apply.

This is a report prepared by the Inter-Faith Consultative Group of the General Synod's Board of Mission for the Church of England in England. It follows other work on the Christian understanding of a religiously plural society in *Towards a Theology for Inter-Faith Dialogue* (1984), '*Multi-Faith Worship*'? (1992), and the Doctrine Commission's recent report *The Mystery of Salvation* (especially chapter 7), although the latter was published after our own document had been completed. Our report deals explicitly with Church of England churches and church halls. There are other considerations which apply to school, college, hospital and other chapels which we could not detail here, although many of the principles noted here will apply in those situations also.

Finally, we have taken advice from the legal officers of the General Synod about the precise situation of canon law as it stands at present, and this information has been incorporated into our report at sections 7.132 and 8.138–8.141. Readers will note, however, that our recommendations go beyond the strict interpretation of canon law to reflect a new situation which was never envisaged by those who framed the present regulations. Canon law is rightly and inevitably based on the experience of the past and cannot be in the vanguard of thought and experiment, where new situations may require new ways of being the people of God. Our hope is that the text which follows provides the right balance of theological affirmation and exploration needed to help us share boldly and faithfully in the mission of God in England today.

+ Thomas Leicester

31 July 1995   *Chairman of the Board of Mission*

1

Disposal and use of church buildings

Facing new questions

1.1   This report brings together two related but different issues concerning church property and other faith communities. They can best be summed up in two imaginary case-studies. The first concerns the *use* of church property:

> The Ravidasis, a community loosely associated with the Sikhs, worship in a former chapel originally bought from a Baptist congregation. One night their temple is destroyed by fire, certainly by arson, probably from racist motives. The Ravidasis approach the local Anglican priest, their nearest worshipping neighbour, to ask if they might use the church hall for worship while their own building is being rebuilt.

1.2   The second concerns the *disposal* of church property:

> St Matthias's is a church with a dwindling congregation and no money for the extensive repairs needed to its fabric. It is decided to sell the building. Two offers come in immediately. One is from a commercial company which plans to pull down the building and replace it with a supermarket. The other is from a group of Bangladeshi Muslims who have been using a private house as their mosque, and have long wanted larger premises. There is no other Christian congregation in the area who might want to buy the building.

1.3   Such situations, and a dozen variations on them, face the Church of England in rural, suburban and inner-city areas. Although Hindus, Muslims and Sikhs in England have acquired or built many of their own buildings in the last few decades, they still frequently experience a need for larger or more appropriate premises, if only on a temporary basis. In 1985 the authors of the report *Faith in the City* wrote:

> It has been obvious to us in our visits to UPAs (urban priority areas) that Christians have far more church buildings than they now need,

and that those they have are often far too large for their purposes. Equally obvious has been the fact that people of other faiths are often exceedingly short of places in which to meet and worship.

Yet the authors of the same report noted that the Church of England has found it extremely difficult to come to a common mind on these issues. Meanwhile, they observed,

> If you are in great need of a place to worship and you see the local Christian church closed most days of the week, and, when it is used, having only a small group of worshippers in just the building that could house your congregation, you are almost bound to feel a sense of rejection if there is a refusal to share. (p. 145)

1.4 A 'common mind' about sharing the use of church buildings with those of other faiths has so far eluded the Church of England. We shall see in chapter 6 that even sharing in this way with fellow-Christians has created difficulties on both sides. Proposals for sharing the same church premises, however infrequently, with Hindus, Jews, Muslims or Sikhs, raise questions about the nature of the faith concerned, its relationship with Christianity, and precisely what activities will be involved. In particular there has been no agreement yet about whether such use is compatible with Christian faith.

1.5 The reasons for redundancy in church buildings may be the ambitious over-provision of churches in the Victorian era, the movement of people from once densely populated areas, or simply a decline in church attendance. Whatever the reasons, the difficulties for the Church of England in deciding on the proper use or disposal of its buildings are theological, legal and emotional – all of them significant. A sense of continuity and history; a gratitude to past generations and to Christian fellow-worshippers now long dead; a desire to maintain a visible symbol of Christian presence in an area which may have undergone many radical changes – these are not feelings to be belittled. For older people especially it can be a painful experience to relinquish years of Christian belonging in one place, and acknowledge that the time has come to move on. This would be likely to happen even if the new users of the building were Christians of a different culture and tradition, but the sense of discontinuity is bound to be sharper when the newcomers are of another faith altogether.

We seem, however, to be in a situation where pain is bound to be felt somewhere. To quote the authors of *Faith in the City* once more:

We have been made aware of the strength of feeling caused by the Church of England's unwillingness to sell redundant churches to other faiths. In many inner-city areas land shortage and planning restrictions prevent either new building or conversion of domestic property. The Church of England is *seen* as possessing a resource of which it can no longer make use, but which it prefers to sell to developers rather than permit members of another faith to use for worship. (p. 152)

1.6   One result of these powerful feelings has been a series of inconclusive debates in the General Synod and elsewhere which are outlined in chapter 2. These have generally addressed only the issue of the sale or long-term leasing arrangements of church property to people of other faiths, but almost equally controversial are the proposals by local congregations to enter into agreements which allow their churches, or (more usually) church halls and other buildings, to be used on a regular or occasional basis by people of other faiths for activities which include worship. Both issues involve the emotional, legal, theological and spiritual significance of churches and other buildings associated with the Church. We need to ask: is that significance solely dependent on continued use, so that it ceases when Christian activity and worship cease there? This would make the building rather like an electrical appliance which is nothing more than an arrangement of plastic and metal once it is unplugged from the current. Another possibility is that the power and effectiveness of Christian life somehow seep into the stones and fabric of the place of Christian worship, making it a place which speaks of holiness. In that case its destruction or ownership by people who stand for things inimical to Christian faith would be felt to be deeply, even shockingly, inappropriate.

1.7   We need to remember that many lives have been lost in conflicts over religious buildings. Muslims have no explicitly sacramental theology, and often say that the whole world is a mosque (see section 4.93), yet they were deeply distressed by the destruction of the mosque at Ayodhya. It was, of course, allegedly built on the site of the birthplace of Rama, which was sacred to Hindus. So one sense of the sacred conflicts with another. Similarly, Carmelite nuns found they had offended some of the deepest feelings of Jewish survivors of the Holocaust when they tried to establish a permanent place of prayer on the site of Auschwitz. Here again, two theologies were in conflict. Christians were attempting to redeem what, in Jewish eyes, could only remain desolate and God-forsaken as a witness to the horror of what had happened there.

3

1.8   Our reference to events outside England are potent reminders that decisions about religious buildings cannot be treated as if they had only local significance. Religious buildings are a symbol and focus of communal identity, and as such, news about them travels far and wide. A number of churches in Britain have been sold to other faith communities, and this has sometimes given the impression in other parts of the world that Christians in Britain are losing ground numerically to Muslims, Sikhs and Hindus. In fact the Church of England has only sold one consecrated church building to members of another faith, but it has leased and sold some dedicated church buildings, which do not have the legal status of consecration, as well as a number of church halls, vicarages and other church property. In some cases Anglicans have also made their buildings available for use by Hindus, Muslims and Sikhs who do not have adequate premises of their own. Neither the practice of selling nor of sharing is easily understood by Christians in those parts of the world where holding the Christian faith is costly, especially where Christians have suffered persecution at the hands of believers of other faiths. Others would defend such practices, however, as examples of good practice in relations between the faiths, and a basis for positive reciprocal treatment by other faith communities in other parts of the world.

1.9   The international dimension of Christian belonging has another aspect. In a rapidly changing society it is tempting to regard church buildings in a purely utilitarian way, valuing them only for their current usefulness as mere containers of worship and other Christian activity. An older tradition which is very much alive in many places sees such buildings as sacramental in character, visible and tangible expressions of Christian faith. Viewed in this way, they are not disposable assets, but require a proper loyalty because they embody in themselves the Christian community's life and history.

1.10   We believe it is vital that the Church of England comes to a clear policy decision about the use and disposal of its church buildings. The Decade of Evangelism focuses attention not only on the Gospel message of the Church, but also on the way that message is lived out in the day-to-day decisions made in the Church's name. On the one hand, the willingness to offer regular hospitality to another faith community might seem to suggest a Christian community which is careless of the integrity of its faith. On the other hand, it could also be seen as a sign of a Christian community secure enough in its faith literally to open its doors to outsiders who need help in establishing their own way of life and worship. When it comes to disposing of a building which is no longer needed, some very difficult decisions have to be made. The cost of repair and maintenance is often underestimated by potential purchasers from either church or other religious bodies, and in some cases only commercial use is financially viable. This may require the total destruction of the building. Some Christians may prefer a former church building to become the site of a car park or a supermarket rather than that it should continue to be used for some other purpose. It is sometimes claimed that a secular use is at least a religiously neutral one. But is it? Perhaps a place of prayer is something to be honoured continuously whichever community of faith possesses it.

1.11   In this report we have followed up previous work published in *Towards a Theology for Inter-Faith Dialogue* (2nd edn. 1986) and *'Multi-Faith Worship'?* (1992) by setting out the course of discussion on the subject within the British Churches for the last 25 years (chapter 2); asking how the Scriptures may speak to us about it (chapter 3); and outlining how Christians have thought through history about holy place and property (chapter 4). We have reviewed how people of other faiths themselves understand sacred space, and what they are looking for in acquiring a building (chapter 5), and noted the experience of English churches in sharing buildings with other Christian Church bodies and the relevant practice of other Christian denominations (chapter 6). We have made our recommendations about disposal (chapter 7) and about use (chapter 8), and finally offered a short bibliography.

2

Debates and decisions within the British Churches 1971-1984

2.12   It is important that in such a controversial area we do not neglect the work of our predecessors, who gave much thought to the questions of church property and other faith communities over two decades ago. We have found, in fact, that most of the current arguments are already set out in their publications and debates. What follows, then, is a record of those discussions.

Five documents

2.13   In 1971 a Working Party was set up by the British Council of Churches with the following terms of reference:

> To seek evidence of the policies and practices of Churches, both centrally and locally, in regard to making church properties in multi-racial areas available for community activities (including policies and practices relating to the disposal of redundant property) and to report to the Board of the Community and Race Relations Unit with a view to the issue of an advisory publication.

In September 1972 this Working Party produced an interim report entitled *The Use of Church Properties for Community Activities in Multi-Racial Areas.* This was followed by their final report, *The Community Orientation of the Church,* in 1974. The Working Party also engaged the services of a sociologist, Ann Holmes, 'to direct surveys designed to produce evidence relevant to our task' in Bradford, Derby and the London Borough of Lambeth. Her research was published in a separate document entitled *Church, Property and People* (BCC, 1973) but arrived too late to receive proper consideration in the final report. In the same year a Working Group of General Synod produced a *Memorandum of Comment* (GS 135) on the interim report. Finally in 1980 the British Council of Churches noted a document it had commissioned to monitor progress of action taken in the light of its three reports mentioned above. This was *The Use of Church Property in a Plural Society.*

2.14   Together, these five documents form a substantial body of work on the use of church properties by people of other faith communities, and on the disposal of such properties when they are redundant. Twenty years have elapsed since four of them were published and this means that our context is now somewhat different, but while we must take account of these changes it would be foolish to ignore this earlier work.

The interim report: *The Use of Church Properties for Community Activities in Multi-Racial Areas* (BCC, 1972)

2.15   The British Council of Churches' Working Party took evidence from 120 witnesses, corporate and individual, from a wide range of Churches. This evidence included 36 papers from local situations and more than 50 letters and papers of theological comment. The report is divided into two parts.

In the first part the following recommendations are made in the light of material received (the numbering is ours, they make many other recommendations which are not relevant to our purposes):

> 1. We recommend as an overriding consideration, Churches with premises should demonstrate to the full their particular fellowship with and care for minority Christian groups (such as the so-called Black Churches) in need of places of assembly for their worship and/or other purposes, by making churches and other premises available to them, even when this involves financial sacrifice by the host community.

2.16   The authors then move on to questions of use by those of other faiths, making careful distinctions about types of church property:

> 2. We recommend that buildings devoted to regular Christian worship should not be made available for the acts of worship of other faiths, whilst recognising . . . the need to consider possible exceptions on their merits.

> 3. We recommend that buildings owned by Churches and used for purposes other than regular Christian worship should be made available to those of other faiths for their worship as well as for their social purposes.

7

4. We recommend that where, in multi-purpose church premises there is a clear distinction between an area devoted to regular Christian worship and the other parts of the building, paragraphs 2 and 3 should apply to the respective areas.

5. We recommend that multi-purpose church premises, used both for regular Christian worship and for other purposes, but with no area devoted solely to Christian worship, should be made available for the social activities of adherents of other faiths, including occasions when an incidental religious rite is involved, such as saying grace at a meal, or an act of individual prayer demanded at a particular hour.

2.17   On the question of disposal the report is unambiguous:

6. We recommend that premises which, having been used for regular Christian. worship, are declared redundant and stripped of Christian symbols, should be made available on appropriate terms to those of other faiths for any purpose for which they may require them.

The report adds that 'the Working Party feels that if necessary such (i.e. redundant) premises should be made available for the worship purposes of other faiths in preference to (say) commercial use, and on other favourable terms'.

7. We recommend that after careful enquiry to establish the facts, churches should, when necessary, exercise the right to decline the use of their premises to groups indulging in derogatory misrepresentation of the Christian faith for propaganda purposes, and to those intending to practise on the premises grosser forms of worship.

2.18   The Working Party also found itself drawn into considering 'dialogue and inter-faith services'. The positions on these issues which are sketched out in the report are still with us, but our concern here is only with buildings.

2.19   There is a note of urgency and impatience throughout the report, for instance in the recommendation that

Churches should call for sacrificial living and giving, and undertake redeployment of resources, on a scale not yet attempted, so as *inter alia* to respond more creatively and extensively to the needs and opportunities of the urban–industrial multi-racial areas . . . Legal and other restrictions upon rapid progress in the direction indicated should be exposed as a first step towards their removal.

In fact government and local authorities have imposed more restrictions since 1972 rather than removing them.

2.20   In a notable anticipation of the *Faith in the City* report a final recommendation says:

> the programme of use of church premises in multi-racial, multi-faith areas should be such that it reflects the commitment of those immediately concerned and, through them, the wider Christian fellowship, to action with their neighbours of other faiths and of none for the common good; and particularly to seek ways of affirming with them our common humanity, and involvement in the struggle for justice, brotherhood and peace. Thus community action groups, day care centres and other such contemporary activities should be among those accommodated in church premises not as 'outsiders', but on terms indicating that they are welcomed equally with the traditional range of church ancillary organisations.

2.21   The second part of the report consists of a paper by John Prickett, Secretary of the Education Department of the British Council of Churches, entitled 'Let These Stones Live'. In this he summarised the vast quantity of submissions received and drew the conclusions on which the report's recommendations were eventually based. Logically, therefore, the second part of the report precedes the first. Not surprisingly Prickett found three positions taken in the submissions, positions which we would now call exclusivism, inclusivism and pluralism. Prickett also summarised the 50 letters and papers of specifically theological comment on the issue of the community use of church property. He noted:

2.22   The letting or selling of church premises for the purposes of worship that is not Christian was the practical problem for most of the writers. For Anglicans in particular there was the somewhat narrower question as to whether there are any circumstances in which it would be proper for a church 'consecrated for Christian worship' to be used for worship that is not Christian.

9

Yet many of his Anglican correspondents were uneasy with the notion of 'consecration' and the legal problems it created. He suggested that there was need for a review of its significance and practice.

2.23   He drew attention to J. G. Davies' book *The Secular Use of Church Buildings* (SCM, 1968) and on its basis gave a useful survey of historical attitudes towards the use of church buildings. He quoted Professor Geoffrey Lampe, who was reminded by Stephen's speech in Acts 7 to ask the question: 'Is it not people and not places which are the "dwelling place of God"?' Referring to Davies, Prickett continued:

> while the early Christian basilica was viewed 'as just another meeting hall with religious overtones', the influence of the OT, especially the comparison with Solomon's Temple, with its holy of holies, and the desire to venerate the tombs of the martyrs by making of them 'holy Shrines', led to the predominance of the idea that the church was a holy place.

2.24   Yet it was used for other purposes than worship. These included, for example: living and sleeping, eating and drinking, dancing, the sale of goods, meetings and legal proceedings, the distribution of poor relief, the playing of games, and acting. Davies suggested that this mixture of activities represented a real synthesis between faith and life, but Prickett questioned his view because what he described occurred not with the blessing of, but in spite of, ecclesiastical authority, which condemned it. And, Prickett asked, was the reason that all these things happened in church actually dictated by the simple fact that there was no other large enough building available?

2.25   As Prickett stated: after the Reformation, the Roman Catholics and Anglicans held to the ideas 'that a church is a holy place and that Solomon's temple was its prototype'. The Puritans,on the other hand, 'steadfastly refused to endorse the concept of specially holy objects or spaces' and sought to replace it by the earlier Christian concept of the holy people. After this historical survey Prickett added that, in recent times: 'holiness, as applied to people, places and things, is increasingly being understood, not to mean "set apart" from the world, but functionally, as God-relatedness in the world.' He continued: 'The practical question of the use of redundant churches by adherents of other faiths may turn (as Professor Moule suggests) very largely on this sacramental principle.'

2.26 Prickett gave some more quotations from the evidence submitted to him, among them a sentence from Professor Maurice Wiles: 'The fundamental issue is whether Muslim or Hindu worship are to be regarded as fundamentally inconsistent with Christian worship.'

2.27 Drawing on Rudolf Otto's book *The Idea of the Holy* (1950), Max Warren, former General-Secretary of the Church Missionary Society, pointed out in his submission that all religions have at their heart a sense of the numinous. The United Reformed Church scholar Martin Cressey suggested that the key point is how the numinous is characterised. Warren felt that Muslim and Hindu worship is not fundamentally inconsistent with Christian worship, while Cressey disagreed.

2.28 Finally, a 'repeated refrain' of the material Prickett examined is the insistence on generosity towards other faith communities: 'We need a theology of hospitality, of generosity, of vulnerability – rather than impregnability.'

The final report: *The Community Orientation of the Church* (BCC, 1974)

2.29 This was published in 1974, after 27 months' work. Besides the report itself, this booklet contains three appendices for us to note: A 'The Recommendations'; B 'The Churches' Response to the interim report' (by Kenneth Sansbury); and C 'A Theological and Pastoral Assessment' (also by Kenneth Sansbury).

2.30 The final report draws attention to a point made in the interim report that 'too little attention has been paid to the psychological aspects of religious conservatism . . . a study would be likely to reveal intimate relation to the use made of church properties'. John Prickett produced a paper on this but 'this subject matter arrived too late for satisfactory conclusion'. The British Council of Churches was asked to produce a 'publication for educational purposes' on this issue.

2.31 The final report accepts the seven recommendations which we have quoted from the interim report, but with a more cautious version of number 3:

> Church premises other than areas devoted to regular Christian worship should be made available to those of other faiths for their social purposes. Those who can do so conscientiously, legally and with pastoral responsibility should also make such premises available to people of other faiths for their religious purposes.

11

2.32   In appendix B Bishop Kenneth Sansbury, General-Secretary of the BCC, summarised the Churches' response to the interim report. The gist of his summary is contained in his own words of introduction:

> The concept of holiness in relation to buildings, the deep-seated psychological attachment to a place linked to the great turning-points of human experience, passionate attachment to the Gospel as the divinely provided way of salvation through Jesus Christ for all mankind, fear of action that might be interpreted by Christians, adherents of other faiths and the indifferent, as 'regarding one religion as good as another' or as 'lowering the flag' – all these tell in one direction. Belief that holiness is a quality of the people of God who here on earth have no abiding city and that over-attachment to bricks and mortar falls below the standard of the New Testament, a conviction that God has not left himself without witness in the other major faiths even though he has revealed his glory uniquely in the face of Jesus Christ, sensitivity to unhappy factors in past relations between Christians and adherents of other faiths (e.g. the Crusades, and the ambiguous links between nineteenth-century missionary and colonial expansion) and a consequent belief that the first duty of Christians to non-Christians in multi-racial areas is to be found in loving service – these tell in the other direction.

2.33   In his description of the Anglican response Sansbury described how General Synod become directly involved in the debate: in May 1972 Wakefield Diocesan Synod asked General Synod to 'debate the principle of the use of consecrated buildings which have been declared redundant'. This request arose because local Muslims had asked to have the use of the redundant and closed St Mary's Dewsbury. General Synod waited to respond to this until the interim report had been published so that it could have a full-scale debate on the whole subject. This took place in February 1973 when General Synod passed a resolution recommending the Church of England where possible to transfer buildings it no longer needed to other Christian Churches that wanted them. It then passed an amendment 'accepting the principle that redundant churches without historical or architectural merit should be demolished and the site sold on the open market if desired'.

2.34   Since these two motions contradicted each other the session was suspended for half an hour so that Standing Committee could try to sort out the procedural confusion. A new form of words was proposed for the July (1973) session of General Synod. This stated that redundant churches 'should not be made available for the purposes of a non-Christian religious faith'.

Sansbury added:

> It was felt that this was what the majority in the February debate had wanted to say. However, Synod defeated this form of words and so in the end refrained from committing itself one way or another on this issue.

Upon which Mr Derek Pattinson, then Secretary-General of the General Synod, commented with characteristic Anglican restraint: 'it is not easy for people outside the Synod, or even for those of us who serve it, to interpret this.'

2.35   Kenneth Sansbury's 'A Theological and Pastoral Assessment' (appendix C) extends over 24 pages. He took as his starting point two statements from the responses to the interim report:

> The questions about the use of buildings are subsidiary to larger questions about attitudes towards people of other faiths and relationships with them.

> Do these questions . . . arise because people think of the preaching of the Gospel as 'the handing over of a doctrinally tight package of theological argument', and religious practice 'as a number of activities confined in the main within the four walls of certain consecrated buildings'?

2.36   This made Sansbury go back to the question: 'how should we think of the faith and mission of the Church today?' There follows a section in which he referred to John Hick (whose book *God and the Universe of Faiths* (1973) had been recently published), Max Warren, Douglas Webster, Karl Rahner, Dom Bede Griffiths, Professor J. N. D. Anderson, and Hans Küng. Sansbury ended this essay by quoting with approval from Ann Holmes' report:

> At the end of the day the question seems to be not, 'What should we do with our buildings?' but 'What is our role as a local church?' After that comes the question, 'What buildings (if any) do we need for the fulfilment of that role?' And after that, 'If our present plant is partly or

13

wholly unsuited to the role agreed, what decisions must we make, in faithfulness to the Gospel and in recognition of the priorities in our localities, about the uses to which it should be put?'

Church, Property and People (BCC, 1973)

2.37   In this document Ann Holmes presented the results of her sociological study, commissioned by the Working Party, 'of the attitudes of churches to their property in three multi-racial, multi-faith areas: Bradford, Derby and Lambeth'. As one would expect from such a survey, the booklet consists largely of a mass of information about local attitudes and responses in the areas concerned. Holmes pointed to a large amount of under-used property which in her opinion often wrongly dictated the pattern of local church life. At the end of her report she said: 'the main problem in connection with redundancy is not so much one of formal restrictions, but of a defensiveness born of the equation of church as property and church as faith or community of believers'.

Memorandum of Comment (GS 135, 1973)

2.38   This document was the one specifically Anglican piece of work to come from this period. It was produced by a Working Party set up by the Standing Committee of General Synod. The Working Party was chaired by Professor Geoffrey Lampe. The other members were the Secretaries of the Board for Mission and Unity, the Board for Social Responsibility, and the Council for Places of Worship.

2.39   The Memorandum, which is a response to the interim report, begins by pointing out that the report goes much further than the Synod debate in 1972 which considered only the use of redundant churches. It recommends that Synod, in returning to the subject, should be similarly comprehensive in its discussion. The Working Party ascertained the views of the missionary societies and sought 'to carry further in certain respects the discussion which (the interim report) has opened'.

2.40   It identifies three distinct areas of Anglican concern:

1. Holiness as a theological concept.

2. The deeply rooted instincts of reverence which people have, quite regardless either of the theological understanding of holiness or of the legal status of the building in question.

3. The legal concepts of consecration and dedication and the consequences which flow from them.

2.41   The document suggests that holiness consists in use and cannot, as it were, be conveyed as a permanent quality. Thus the notion of consecration in perpetuity rests on shaky theological foundations. (See section 2.21 for other reservations on the whole notion of the consecration of buildings.):

> It is important, we believe, to try to distinguish Christian concern for the holiness, at second remove, of a building as a place used for the service of God by his holy people, from the sacredness with which even a semi-Christian 'tribal' religion may invest it.

On the different attitudes towards the use of church properties it says:

> For one group in this situation their concern with community is essentially a concern with development, bringing into existence that which as yet exists only fitfully and in the face of pressures towards disintegration . . . For other groups in the same situation what is at issue is the continued existence of a community seen as a pattern of life, something received and shared in the face of changes and additions which are experienced as threats.

2.42   It comes down in principle on the same side of the debate as the interim report had done: 'sharing buildings for social purposes and, in appropriate cases, making church buildings available to other faiths need not be seen as a shameful capitulation, a retreat in the face of the forces of disintegration in society.' At no point does this Memorandum significantly dissent from the interim report.

The Use of Church Property in a Plural Society (BCC, 1980)

2.43   This points out that the practice of local churches has moved on. It also points out the confusion caused by the wide variety of legal provision affecting different churches. 'One church may have a much larger measure of control or discretion in the disposal of its buildings than another.' It comments that, 'Under the Pastoral Measure 1968 the Church of England has considerable freedom in the disposal of redundant buildings', and says 'it would be beneficial if the other churches could enjoy a similar freedom'. Because of the legal confusion it suggests that a central advice centre should be set up.

The Synod Debate of 1983

2.44   In the context of the proposal to sell a consecrated Anglican church in Southampton to the Sikh community another debate took place in General Synod in February 1983 at the request of the Church Commissioners, who have the final responsibility for decisions about the disposal of church property. The motion was that 'church buildings which have been declared redundant may in appropriate circumstances be made available to those of non-Christian faiths for the purpose of their worship'. Voting on this more restricted motion took place as in 1973 in houses, and it was carried in the House of Bishops and narrowly in the House of Clergy, but lost as before in the House of Laity, this time by 96–90.

2.45   The speeches reflected this deep division on the subject. All seemed to agree that holiness was determined by use, rather than being intrinsic to the fabric of the building, but there was deep disagreement about the pastoral effect of a willingness to hand over churches to those of other faiths. Those in favour of the motion appealed for generosity to ethnic minorities not only in word but in deed, and some said that the real divide in our society was between the spiritual and the non-spiritual. The Bishop of Winchester (John V. Taylor) stated that there were two traditions in the Christian Scriptures; one addressed to those tempted to apostasy, which denied the existence of other gods and warned against the demonic, and another addressed to the religiously complacent which warned that the children of the Kingdom would be displaced by those coming from East and West. None of the opponents of the motion, who were primarily concerned about sowing confusion and appearing to abandon Christian mission, had any proposal about what should be done with a church building which was not needed either by the Church of England or any other Christian body. Some clearly preferred to see it demolished, and then perhaps the site sold to another faith community. If it became a supermarket, it was said, that was at least a neutral use. This reflected an anxiety about a former church building being used for purposes which were thought to be anti-Christian (though these were not defined), and it was argued that it was impossible to find safeguards in such a case, or to draw lines between different kinds of faith community.

The Church Commissioners' Guidelines

2.46   After this rather inconclusive debate the Church Commissioners in June 1984 drew up guidelines for the procedures to be followed when another religious body is interested in acquiring (under the Pastoral Measure 1983) an Anglican church building by purchase or lease and using it for worship. They are as follows, dealing first with Christian groups:

> Where a religious body has shown interest in using a redundant church, special care should be taken to consider the matter before the body concerned is encouraged to feel that they will be allowed to have the building. As regards use for worship by bodies other than the Church of England, the following guidance can be given:

(i) Use as a place for worship by Christian bodies which are members or associate members of, or official observers at the British or the World Council of Churches would ordinarily be regarded assuitable.

(ii) There is a *prima facie* case for accepting, as suitable, use as a place of worship by Christian bodies which though qualified to be members of the British or the World Council of Churches are not members, but each application has to be considered on its merits.

(iii) Use for worship by a body claiming to be Christian and not coming under either (i) or (ii) above should not automatically be ruled out of consideration. But a diocesan uses committee, after making enquiries into the beliefs and practices of the religion concerned and with due regard to the particular local circumstances, would be well advised to consult the Commissioners on such a proposal at an early stage.

2.47 They then come to disposal to other faith communities:

(iv) In the light of the unique revelation of God in Jesus Christ, use for worship by adherents of a non-Christian faith is not to be regarded as an evidently suitable use which a diocesan uses committee should seek or prefer to other types of use. If, nevertheless, a case arises where the committee with the clear support of the Bishop would wish the Commissioners to consider such a proposal, then, in such a case, the Commissioners will judge the suitability of the proposed use on its merits taking into account all the relevant circumstances. These will include:

(a) the belief, practices and attitudes to the Christian Church of the particular non-Christian body as manifested both locally and in other parts of the world;

(b)   the historic and architectural nature and importance of the redundant building and its contents; the effect of any structural alterations needed to facilitate the proposed use; and the general significance of the building in the local and wider Christian community;

(c)   the views of the Anglican and other Christian congregations and bodies in the locality (N.B. in the former case the views of the parochial church council and the deanery synod should follow debates on clearly expressed motions with votes being taken.);

(d)   the view of the MP, the local authorities and other representative figures; and the views of the local residents so far as these have been made known;

(e)   the availability or prospect of other alternative uses for the redundant building, especially use by another Christian denomination.

2.48   The guidelines conclude:

When the Commissioners have before them all the relevant information concerning a specific proposal, they will be able to decide whether a draft redundancy scheme to give effect to this proposal should be published. If they do so decide, their final decision on whether or not to submit the scheme for confirmation by Order in Council cannot be taken until they have considered, after consultation with the Bishop, any representations received during the 28 days statutory notice period.

Conclusion

2.49   In the ten years since this interim resolution of the issue only one consecrated Anglican church, St Luke's Southampton, has been sold to another faith community, the Sikhs. This proposal was the occasion, though not the subject, of the 1983 debate. The issue, however, like the parallel one of the use of church buildings by those of other faiths, has not gone away. In fact new situations are being created in the chapels of hospitals, colleges and other institutions like airports and prisons, where there is a demand that Muslims and others share their use. In some places a new chapel or religious area is proposed and the question arises as to how it may be constructed to serve a multi-religious community. However, we shall not in this report attempt to deal with these new situations, which are invariably the responsibility of ecumenical Christian groups, though we hope the principles we describe will facilitate their decisions. Our concern here is with church buildings owned by the Church of England.

3

How do the Scriptures
help us decide?

3.50   As we turn to the Bible for guidance about holiness, worship, buildings, consecration and related issues we are faced by two immediate questions:

> 1. How do we relate the Bible to our present situation about church buildings and other faith communities when Scripture contains no reference to a church building and when both the Old and New Testament deal with situations very different from our own?

> 2. What do we expect from Scripture in seeking help on complex issues related to the interface between Christianity and other faiths when Christians hold such differing views among themselves?

Clearly, there are no ready-made answers to the many modern questions and complexities which confront us in this area. We have to look first of all for guidance about the way in which the authors of Scripture understood the significance of sacred space and holy buildings. In doing this we can also discover clues which, to differing degrees, help us in deciding how our stewardship of them should be exercised. In the process of this exploration the Bible yields vital principles and precedents. As it demonstrates different contexts and perspectives we are helped in answering the questions which are posed by our situation today, always mindful that God is not limited by his actions in the past while being consistent and coherent in all his action within history. But in many contemporary questions the Scriptures *help* us to decide. They do not decide for us.

3.51   The other related, and much larger question which we bring to the Scriptures in this context is how to regard the desire of other faith communities to pray and worship. Our understanding of this will go far in determining our answer to questions about the proper use of our buildings. The Board of Mission has tackled this question previously, especially in *'Multi-Faith Worship'?* (GS 1011, 1992). Here also Scripture is applicable to our circumstances only by careful analogy: Hinduism and Buddhism lay beyond the knowledge of the authors of Scripture, and the great figures of Islam and Sikhism lived and taught long after the canon of Scripture was closed. Again we have to work by principle and precedent. Other faith communities surrounded Israel, serving as both a threat and as a warning. To Israelites tempted by foreign worship they stood as a sign of what happens when the covenant was broken and God's blessing lost. To Israelites arrogantly secure in their conviction of God's favour they were the people who threatened to displace them in that very favour. In the New Testament the social context is the minority status of the small group of Christian believers within the Jewish community and within the Roman Empire.

3.52   Returning to the more specific concerns of Christian buildings and other faith communities, it is necessary to begin by looking at some of the Old Testament references to holiness of place. It is helpful to see these in the theological context of Genesis 1–11 which provides the setting for the whole Torah. Here we note that *holiness* is an attribute of time rather than of physical space. The sabbath indicates an idea of holiness that is specially focused by a particular length of time. Many faith communities have a sense of holy time and observe a calendar of sacred fast and festival which is determined among Hindus and Muslims by the moon. Muslims gather together particularly on Friday, Jews on Saturday and Christians on Sunday. Alongside the idea of buildings as a focused locus of God's presence and holiness we recognise a structure in time which proclaims similar truths. We are dealing with something fundamental to humanity's apprehension of God: in seeking God and responding to his holiness we require recognisable foci.

Genesis

3.53   Turning to the stories of the Patriarchs we find a number of situations where there is a particular significance accorded to the place or the building where some event occurs. The earliest 'buildings' were simple forms used for cultic purposes. These were especially sacred pillars or stelae, and rudimentary altars. The purpose of these was presumably to mark both a locus and an event for a relatively short period, a kind of 'X marks the spot': an epiphany takes place at a particular point in time which marks a meeting place between heaven and earth. How long the buildings themselves persisted would depend on the durability of the materials used and the effect of weather. But, as well as creating something material to mark the place, another important facet is the act of naming, or dedication, and this is perhaps more important than the materials used, since this was under the builder's control, whereas the materials had to be whatever came to hand. Dedication means claiming the place and time for God, especially as a testimony or witness to an event.

3.54   The stories of the Patriarchs include some specific illustrations of such cultic practices (e.g. Genesis 8. 20; 12. 7, 8; 13. 4; 16. 10–14; 21. 33; 22. 13–14; 23. 1–20; 26. 25). One of the most significant is Jacob's dream (Genesis 28. 10–22). Here is a vivid description of the joining of earth and heaven and the 'traffic' between them. It is the gate of heaven, marked thus: 'And this stone, which I have set for a pillar, shall be God's house.' The *ritual* associated with the cultic behaviour speaks of an *intention* to *acknowledge* the sacred at this locus, because of the powerfulness of the dream/vision. The dream is transitory, but the power of the revelation endures, and the ritual is set up so that it shall endure, a mark of which is Jacob's renaming of the place, *Bethel*, the House of God. His payment of a tithe may well suggest his endowment of the shrine to ensure its continuation, for however temporary some of these shrines were, there is evidence of continuing sacred importance given to particular places by these theophanies. But, on the whole, these nomadic people make no attempt to perpetuate a worshipping presence or build a house of God as a focus of community worship and response to God. Being landless they have no capacity to do so. The first indication of a move towards the permanent possession of land is in connection with the need for a grave for Sarah, to which the whole of chapter 23 of Genesis is devoted.

The Exodus

3.55   In the Exodus, the emergence of a strongly bonded Israelite community is marked by a change from sporadic occasions of interaction with God to his continuous presence. This is founded on the major encounter at Sinai which becomes the foundation of the covenant between God and his people. 'You brought them in and planted them on the mountain of your own possession, the place, O Lord, that you made your abode, the Sanctuary, O Lord, that your hands have established' (Exodus 15. 17). The Israelites now have a permanent, indestructible symbol of the presence of God among them – the holy mountain. But, since migrant people move, the living God, bound to them in covenant, moves continuously with them. Thus is generated the concept of a sanctuary, the idea of Ark and Tabernacle, which is a movable Sinai; and the general holiness of the whole people is juxtaposed with the specific holiness of some people (the priests) and some places (the Tabernacle). 'And have them make me a sanctuary, so that I may dwell among them' (Exodus 25. 8).

3.56   The instructions for the Ark (which are given by God, and require special craftsmen to be appointed) are interesting in terms of their insistence on precious and pure materials for the purpose of enclosure. If God is elemental, manifesting himself in the form of a pillar of cloud, or a pillar of fire, then his presence is signified by the special nature of what is made by human hands in his honour. The Ark is the circumscriber and sign of the holy presence of God, which yet cannot be transcribed into any solid reality (who can hold fire or cloud in his hand?). Though both Ark and Tabernacle are movable, this mobility and flexibility do not signify any impermanence or provisionality about this focus of God's presence. The eternal significance of the sanctuary is made specific as the *quality* of the covenant is imparted to the receptacle: a permanent light will burn which 'shall be a perpetual ordinance to be observed throughout their generations by the Israelites' (Exodus 27. 21). The Tabernacle, like the mountain, becomes a place of encounter, a meeting point between God and humanity, earth and heaven: 'I will meet with the Israelites there, and it shall be sanctified by my glory.' The human-made becomes theophany through *the glory of the Lord*. The presence of the glory of the Lord confirms the covenant, the belief of the people, and the sense of community.

3.57   Underlying both the holiness of Mount Sinai and the Tabernacle is a communicable sense of power, mystery and awe (Exodus 19. 12, 24); the consecrated altar becomes holy, and whatever touches it also becomes holy (Exodus 29. 37). This means that unqualified people, or those who contravene the sacred regulations, bring disaster on themselves (Leviticus 10. 1–3, cf. the fates of Uzzah in 2 Samuel 6. 7 and King Uzziah in 2 Chronicles 26. 16–21). This transmission works both ways, however, so that there are concomitant concerns about pollution, and steps to be taken so that the Holy of Holies is not polluted. It is necessary to 'reverence my sanctuary' (Leviticus 19. 30; 26. 2). This requires constant examination of all the internal relationships and keeps the community strong and resolute even in adversity. God's people are separate from other peoples (Leviticus 20. 26), and the Levites are separate from the rest of God's people (Numbers 1. 51, 8. 14). When the Israelites enter the Promised Land they are to tear down all altars to other gods (Exodus 34. 13) and burn their images (Deuteronomy 7. 25, 12. 2f.), allowing no sacred pillar to be put beside the altar of the Lord

(Deuteronomy 16. 21f.). Whether such injunctions were observed or not, the principle was clearly that holiness is totally inconsistent with uncleanness and must be protected from profanation; the holy place is the focus and source of both law and ritual; and the presence of the Ark unites the community, where God is permanently present among them. This is a stage in God's relations with his people before their arrogance and injustice brought about their downfall.

The House of God

3.58   With settlement in the Promised Land, there is a new situation, requiring a modified approach to the idea of the sanctuary. Nathan the prophet, in response to King David's expressed desire to build a house for the Ark of God, brings the word of the Lord to him,

> Are you the one to build me a house to live in? I have not lived in a house since the day I brought up the people of Israel from Egypt to this day, but I have been moving about in a tent and a tabernacle. (2 Samuel 7. 5, 6)

This is true and makes sense in context, but times are changing: David's son will build a house for the Lord. Therefore, we can see that the Lord sets his word upon changes specific to new generations and to varying contexts, from nomads (the Patriarchs), to settlers (the nation of Israel), and then to migrants (the Exile). God will reside in the context of his people. There is, therefore, a change of language to meet the new situation. So Solomon is expressing an acceptable response to God in saying, 'I have built you an exalted house, a place for you to dwell in forever' (1 Kings 8. 13). Here, the language of permanency still obtains, but is transferred from the eternal flame to the idea of a permanent house. It has, however, been a significant change, one that causes much theological reflection: 'But will God indeed dwell on the earth? Even heaven and the highest heaven cannot contain you, much less this house that I have built!' (1 Kings 8. 27). This meditation on the import of the acts involved in constructing the Temple reflects on the graciousness of God, who, though infinite, yet allows his presence to reside among his people. This may also be seen as prophetic of the Incarnation, in that God, who cannot be contained, permits himself to enter into space and time and into enclosure, to come among his people. God's response therefore affirms this understanding: 'I have consecrated this house that you have built, and put my name there forever; my eyes and my heart shall be there for all time' (1 Kings 9. 3). The Name and selfhood of God, the identity and nature of God are graciously offered within the temple in perpetuity.

3.59   Reflecting on the details of the Tabernacle and its successor, the Temple, it is important to recognise, within the stress on God dwelling in the midst of a people gathered about him, the notion of a graded holiness culminating in a central point. This is communicated in the architecture and the materials of the Tabernacle, and is taken over by the later Temples (and churches). This idea of grading is taken further by the Rabbinic writers in that they describe ten degrees of holiness from the first degree, which is the land of Israel (a land that is holier than any other land), on through ascending degrees to Jerusalem, the Temple Mount, the various courts of the Temple and the near approaches to the sanctuary, right up to the tenth degree which is the Holy of Holies. This gradation suggests the need to nuance the expressions of holiness as they are reflected in particular buildings and situations.

3.60   The Old Testament shows the struggles of Israel in responding rightly to the presence of God in the Temple. There was a very clear integration of cultic and moral concepts of holiness which was a centrally recurring theme within the message of the prophets. Jeremiah hotly denies that the preservation of the Temple is God's concern at all, in the face of his people's iniquity (chapters 12 and 26). Micah had already said something similar (3. 12). The Temple should be a place where people of all nations come to pray, according to Isaiah (56. 7), but Jeremiah thinks that it has become a den of thieves (7. 11), (to note the double reference made famous by Jesus – Mark 11. 17). In the face of the Exile, voices of hope link the establishment of justice to the re-establishment of a worshipping people. Above all we notice these themes in Jeremiah and Ezekiel who announced the destruction of the Temple by the will of God. In Ezekiel, the glory of God departs from the Temple as Israel shows itself unable to change its ways (Ezekiel 11. 23). There is, thus, a strong theme of the judgement of God on his rebellious people, which ultimately leads to the destruction of their places of worship if his people persist in their rebellion. The holiness of God departs before this destruction, and the tragic irony is that the people do not realise it (Jeremiah 7). Various specific reasons are given for this tragedy in different biblical documents (especially Jeremiah, Ezekiel and Deuteronomy), but the most notable causes are idolatry, pride, injustice and complacency. It is only when Israel accepts this judgement that the promise of a restored Temple can be communicated. The growing importance of moral purity within the Exile, together with visions

25

of the universality of the *missio dei* seem to take precedence over the physical place of cultic holiness:

> Heaven is my throne and the earth is my footstool; what is the house that you would build for me, and what is my resting place? . . . But this is the one to whom I will look, to the humble and contrite in spirit, who trembles at my word. (Isaiah 66. 1, 2)

3.61   Nevertheless, the suffering of the loss of God's house had been a source of immense pain; consequently, the joy at the restoration of the temple should not be underestimated. It is portrayed as God's act of rebuilding and re-establishing his people for their mission in the world. This is well portrayed through the strength of the decree of King Darius about the rebuilding of the Temple: 'May the God who has established his name overthrow any king or people that shall put forth a hand to alter this, or to destroy this house of God in Jerusalem' (Ezra 6. 12). Alongside this must be put the voice of the prophets who speak of the results that will follow the restoration of the Temple, as in Haggai: 'Go up to the hills and bring wood and build the house, so that I may take pleasure in it and be honoured, says the Lord' (1. 8). Beyond this, the restoration opens up the future for the *whole* fulfilment of the Lord's promises.

> I will shake all nations, so that the treasure of all nations shall come, and I will fill this house with splendour . . . The latter splendour of this house shall be greater than the former, says the Lord of hosts; and in this place I will give prosperity. (Haggai 2. 7, 9)

The act of restorative building provides the context for hope in the culmination of God's promises, and, in a Messianic context, the extension of those promises to social and political conditions: 'On that day, says the Lord of hosts, you shall invite each other to come under your vine and fig tree' (Zechariah 3. 10). They look forward to what has been prophesied by Micah who foresees many nations coming to Jerusalem and saying, 'Come, let us go up to the mountain of the Lord, to the House of the God of Jacob; that he may teach us his ways and that we may walk in his paths' (Micah 4. 1–3). Here, instead of looking inwards for protection, there is a boldly outward-looking and inclusive vision.

3.62   Following the return from Exile, the notion of gathering together in synagogues developed as a feature within Israel's understanding of holy places. Where stability is established, the place of worship can be multiplied as a focus for each discrete community. However, the archaeological evidence suggests that synagogues were either multifunctional meeting places or, possibly, mobile Torah shrines. They were offshoots of the central holy place, Jerusalem and its Temple, and as such are functional places of local importance and use which are dependent on Jerusalem.

3.63   In this brief exploration of some of the relevant Old Testament material it is possible to see a linear progression in the understanding of the *house of God.*

> Phase 1. Cultic places which are local intersections of heaven and earth, restricted in space and time.

> Phase 2. The Ark and Tabernacle which speak of God on the move in the midst of his people following their calling to be his chosen people, consolidated in the presence of his glory.

> Phase 3. The Temple with the presence of God's holiness finding its permanent locus within the sanctuary in Jerusalem from where it radiates outwards.

> Phase 4. Plural places which are Torah shrines, places of local worship and offering, in addition (and sometimes rivalry) to the central focus of Jerusalem to which they were oriented.

It is important to see this development not so much as a progressive rejection of former ideas and practices which were now considered invalid but, rather, as evidence of the evolving nature of ideas of holy place appropriate to the particular situation. As such, they provide clues for the wide range of differing situations in which we may find ourselves today.

New Testament

3.64   When we turn to the New Testament, we have to remember the minority context in which the authors wrote. We note a continuation of the prophetic call for a re-evaluation and reinterpretation of what actually *goes on* in the relationship between God, place, and worship:

> 1. In Matthew 12 Jesus shows that the needs of human beings come before a strict application of the Law. David eats the shewbread and basic human hunger is assuaged; the man with the withered hand is healed, despite this being work on the sabbath. Further, this impera-

tive comes from the Son of God in his Father's house who, nevertheless, declares: 'I tell you, something greater than the Temple is here'
(v.6). On this reading, if we wish to follow Christ, we *must* respond to
the legitimate needs of others within the house of God, even if this
appears to go against our deep feelings regarding regulation and holiness. (Cf. Mark 2. 26, 27; 3. 1–15 etc.).

2. Of clear importance is the attitude of Jesus towards the Temple as
well as the early Christian understanding of the relationship between
the person of Christ and the place of the Temple. Jesus's act of purg-
ing the Temple of its moral defilement is in line with the prophetic
challenge to human carelessness and presumption in relation to the
holiness of the Temple. Also, within this tradition, is Jesus's prophecy
that the Temple would soon be overthrown (Mark 13. 1f.), and the
prominence of that threat in his trial (14. 58). Jesus, continuing the
tradition of Jeremiah, was challenging the popular admiration of the
Temple and the reliance on it as the sign of God's protection. This had
once already led to destruction and exile. It is true that the Temple
continues to have a significance for Jesus, his disciples, and for the
Early Church in Jerusalem. Luke begins and ends his Gospel in the
Temple. Nevertheless the primary teaching of the New Testament is
that the presence and glory of God reside in the person of Jesus. After
the resurrection it is the followers of Jesus who constitute a spiritual
house of sacrifice and worship, living stones of which he is the chief
cornerstone (1 Peter 2. 5f.). The whole system of sacrificial offerings
has been superseded by the sacrifice of Christ once and for all. The
implication can only be that the physical Temple is redundant
(Hebrews 8, 9).

3. The story of Jesus and the Samaritan woman in John 4 can be
interpreted in a number of different ways. They meet at a place of cultic significance (Jacob's well) which supplies basic human need. Jesus
encounters this woman of Samaria and enters into dialogue with her.
The woman finds this odd because 'Jews do not share things in common with Samaritans.' But, in sharing water for basic human need at
the place of historical and cultic importance, there is mutual access to
understanding of God: there is 'living water'. Their conversation
begins with the question of place and worship: 'Our ancestors worshipped on this mountain, but you say that the place where people

must worship is in Jerusalem.' Jesus says that the argument about differentiation of locus (cultic place/temple) is irrelevant, since while the *place* of worship varies, the *object* of true worship never changes: 'You worship what you do not know; we worship what we know, for salvation is from the Jews . . . true worshippers will worship the Father in spirit and in truth.' On this understanding that the *worship of the true God* is more important than where it takes place, Jesus reveals himself as the Christ to the Samaritan woman.

4. Jesus challenged formerly held views of ritual holiness. He deliberately touched lepers and went into places regarded as ritually unclean (Mark 7. 24). He was clear that uncleanness comes from the evil within a person, and not from what is encountered in the surrounding environment (Mark 7. 18–23). His trial and crucifixion took place in areas regarded by Jews as contaminated by Gentile presence or by death (John 18. 28, Matthew 27. 33), yet brought about salvation (Galatians 3. 13).

3.65   At the crucifixion the veil of the temple was rent in two, a sign of the power of God in the Incarnate Son. In Christ God confined himself to a human body, but yet cannot be confined to time and place. That is confirmed by the death and resurrection of that body. Henceforth, the presence of God is linked with the bringing in of the Kingdom. In the Kingdom, the *people* are God's presence, and, as the Kingdom is brought in, more and more people become mediators of God's presence. People matter more than place. We are still at this stage of God's mission, until we worship him in the temple-less city of God in the end-time. The decisions we now have to make about the use of our church buildings should depend upon what we think will promote the values of the Kingdom, as we understand them from what has been happening in God's dealings with his people.

3.66   Given the eschatological perspective of the New Testament, it is important to balance our looking back with looking forward:

Then I saw a new heaven and a new earth . . . I saw the holy city, the new Jerusalem, coming down out of heaven from God . . . See, the tabernacle of God is among mortals. He will dwell with them as their God; they will be his peoples, and God himself will be with them. (Revelation 21. 1–3)

Here, again, in the new Jerusalem there is a set of instructive descriptions, but these have become rarified. They are not base, such as earth, metal, stone, but precious: jasper, pure gold, glass. Further, 'I saw no temple in the city, for its temple is the Lord God the Almighty and the Lamb' (21. 22). At the eschaton, the city of God is a total theophany. The glory of God is not just contained in the natural world, but the world *is* glory, and the presence of God permeates all things.

Emerging principles

3.67   One difficulty with the New Testament material in relation to holy places and buildings is its limited corpus and setting. As the early Christians were such a small group of Jews and Gentiles living in the few decades following the earthly life of Jesus, questions of church buildings and their relation to the holy God did not immediately arise. The Book of Acts shows us how synagogues and homes were used by Christians in their worship, and how the latter were the normal place for eucharistic or love-feast meetings. There seems little interest in cultic space or cultic purity (Acts 10. 15). In consequence some Christian traditions have regarded with suspicion the subsequent developments in the area of church building and *holy space* in which much of the thinking has depended on insights from the experience of the people of God in the Old Testament. For them the New Testament emphasis is exclusively on the people of God as holy in a way which leaves no space for any particular places as being more holy than others. But such a view can only be sustained by isolating the New Testament texts from the contexts immediately preceding and following them. Most therefore believe that the development and variety of thought and use of buildings in the Old Testament provide useful parameters for our evolving Christian understanding of holy places as channels for an authentic and positive response to God in worship.

3.68   The most helpful way to look at specific situations today in the light of the Scriptures is to bring the particular issues to the text, within an overall understanding of the development of the biblical perspective, and then to look for principles and clues to show possible directions forward. In general, however, the following principles seem to emerge from a biblical study of these areas:

> 1. The sanctuary of a church and its effects confer a sense of holiness, and of the meeting of earth and heaven. There are certain 'natural' symbols for holiness and the representation of God, such as gold or other precious metals, a linear or central orientation of graded access

to God, an upward movement that again symbolises the exalted God, and a cruciform shape with its particular Christological significance. As a consequence we may well conclude that certain architectural features of church buildings cannot easily be overlaid or changed.

2. Worship uses the building as focus or lens, but God is not confined there, only locally focused. We need not be suspicious of the *holy materialism* that pervades the Bible, and underestimate the importance of the Church's buildings. God is present in his people in the world but in a different mode from what is possible at worship within the sanctuary.

3. The Church is concerned with bringing in the Kingdom after the example of Christ; therefore it will seek to be a local focus for helping people to be part of God's presence for others.

4. History and artistic expression matter and are important in understanding the development of our attitudes towards the use and disposal of buildings, but mission thinking demands a move outwards beyond buildings and static confinements.

5. There are notions of gradation within the concept of holiness which suggest the need for a nuanced approach to different kinds of holy places and the different significance which they have for particular people in specific places at particular times.

6. Holy places can be either temporary or permanent in intention and significance, and, even where originally they were intended to be permanent, they can cease to be *holy places* in the light of fresh developments within the purposes and mission of God It is also possible that the *departure of significance* is an aspect of judgement rather than a new stage in God's pilgrimage with his people.

7. Allowing people of other faiths into the arena of Christian worship (both time and place) affords a witnessing encounter which does not proselytise.

8. The move towards the eschaton and the realisation of theophany is inclusive not exclusive of all who worship in spirit and truth.

9. It seems clear from the teaching and practice of Jesus, in particular, that what matters more than anything else is the *intention* of Christians concerning the use and disposal of their buildings.

4

Meeting, memory, mystery
Perspectives on holy place and property

4.69   However the Scriptures should be understood, today as throughout history most Christians recognise certain places or buildings as being distinctively endowed with religious significance; most people of other faiths do so too, and the singling out of certain places as in some way 'special' is widespread also in the apparent secularity of much modern western culture. Acknowledgement and investigation of this 'sense of place' are clearly important in considering both the use of church buildings by other faith communities and their disposal to those communities.

4.70   In Anglican terminology, the words 'consecration' and 'dedication' refer to two distinct legal and liturgical acts by which such a sense of place may be defined – the term 'hallowing' being sometimes used to cover both. Legally, consecration means: 'setting apart a building for ever exclusively for the service of God', an act reserved in Anglicanism to the bishop. Consecration brings the land or building within the faculty jurisdiction of the consistory court of the diocese. Dedication, on the other hand, has no definite legal significance, may be performed by a priest, and is not thought of as conferring a theoretically indelible character like consecration. It is true, however, that a ceremony known as 'deconsecration' has developed as a liturgical end to the special character of a building once the legal effects of consecration have been removed by the appropriate legal steps (which involve the authority of an Act or a Measure).

4.71   The legal terms clearly embody deeply felt perceptions about sacred places. The underlying psychological, sociological, and spiritual realities which contribute to shaping these individual and ecclesial perceptions can best be indicated through tracing themes in the liturgy of hallowing church buildings. Liturgical patterns also point to theological questions about the meaning of consecrated places which must be addressed in considering their use by or disposal to people of other faiths.

4.72   The post-Reformation Church of England has never authorised an official liturgy for the consecration of a church, though some other Anglican provinces have. In the seventeenth century, a form drawn up by Bishop Lancelot Andrewes was influential, and a simplified version of that was approved by the Convocations in 1712; but royal assent was not received. Andrewes' form was in continuity with medieval and patristic developments in the liturgy, and it is particularly the period which saw the establishment of Christianity as the imperial religion, from the fourth to the sixth centuries, which is formative for those developments. The first recorded consecration of a church building is that described by Eusebius at Tyre in 314. As in all Christian spirituality and theology of this period, it is necessary to bear in mind the rich resources of imagery and symbolism drawn by Christians from the Old Testament. Just as the categories of Aaronic priesthood were applied to elucidating the structure of Christian ministry, so Christian buildings and places were interpreted in the light of the Jewish sense of holy place focused on the Temple. For example, the Christian observance of annual 'Dedication Festivals' probably originated in the fourth-century Jerusalem church in imitation of the Jewish feast of Hanukkah.

4.73   Three important elements can be identified in the development of the liturgy: the celebration of the eucharist, the deposition of relics, and the performance of various rites of purification. These can be related to three different ways in which places came to be used for Christian worship: as houses where the faithful gathered for regular worship, as tombs marking the sites of martyrdom, and as pre-Christian sanctuaries taken over and adapted to a new faith. That in turn is indicative of three different dimensions in the Christian consciousness of the holiness of church buildings: they are *places of meeting*, venues for the assembly of the eucharistic community; they are *places of memory*, sites associated with key stories of the faith; and they are *places of mystery*, environments charged with the presence of the divine. It is also possible to see these three dimensions reflected, in different idioms and with different emphases, in the traditions of other faiths, and in more general secular attitudes to special places. Each aspect raises specific questions in considering the possibility of other-faith use or disposal. Theologically, the three dimensions are interdependent: as the community of faith meets in a place, they invest it with the memories of faith, and discover in it the mystery of faith; equally, as they rehearse the memories or approach the mystery, people become more deeply part of the community. From the point of view of liturgical development, though, it is best to begin with the dimension of 'meeting' – and it is on this alone that much contemporary theology of consecrated places is based.

Places of meeting

4.74   The central element in the consecration liturgy has always been the use of a building for Christian worship. Primarily, this has meant the celebration of the eucharist: Eusebius' account of the earliest dedication at Tyre refers to a eucharist, and Pope Vigilius in 538 explained that a mass, without further ceremonies, was sufficient to consecrate a church without relics. At other times, and particularly within the Anglican tradition, the eucharist has been accompanied by as many as possible of the other offices – some formularies even providing for the burial of the dead to be part of the liturgy.

4.75   This centrality of the eucharist is clearly in continuity with the practice of the Early Church, which met as a eucharistic assembly in the homes of believers without first insisting that those homes should be consecrated. This is a pattern to be found as early as the New Testament, where churches are identified as those 'meeting in the house of' Priscilla and Aquila (Romans 16. 5; 1 Corinthians 16.19) or Nympha (Colossians 4. 15), and the 'breaking of bread on the first day of the week' takes place in the upper chamber of a house in Troas (Acts 20. 7). There were changes in emphasis, though, as the church grew in size. What were originally private dwelling places were made over to the collective ownership of the Christian community as public meeting places. In Rome, evidence of this is provided by the retention of the original owners' names as titles for some of the earliest church buildings. Individual generosity thus provides the basis for corporate hospitality: vestiges of this tradition may be seen in post-Reformation Anglican dedication rites where the liturgy begins with an address made by the donor to the bishop.

4.76   Whether owned by an individual or a community, the church seen as home must be a place both of safety for those who meet there and of hospitality in welcoming others to join that meeting. Fundamentally, one depends on the other: a place which is not secure is not able to offer hospitality to others. In practice, the two requirements may be in tension, and the balance between them will vary from place to place and time to time. In the first centuries, for example, before the community's identity was firmly established and when there was threat of persecution, emphasis was necessarily on the private home as a secure place for the celebration of the secret mysteries of the eucharist – presence there was the badge of Christian identity, safeguarded both by watchers at the door and by the *disciplina arcani* banishing catechumens from the central part of the rite. With growing confidence and external acceptance, the Christians' secure home could be opened up as a place of welcome to strangers, and a meeting point for the entire community. So churches became important public buildings, modelled on the basilicas of classical cities.

4.77   The tension between security and hospitality has surfaced at various times throughout the Church's history. It is certainly a live issue today, for example in the decisions churches must take over locking their doors during weekdays for security or leaving them open for casual visitors; or, still more contentiously, the extent to which they make their church halls available for use by groups from outside the church. Whatever the balance between security and hospitality achieved in the thought and practice of a particular church, the building is here primarily understood as a place for the community to gather. Certainly this is a theological position reflected in the New Testament, the second-century Apologists (e.g. Minucius Felix in *Octavius* 32) and most modern ecumenical thought and practice in the West. According to this view, holiness resides in the churches as people, and the holiness of buildings is derivative merely from their acting as a shell to accommodate the holy people; consecration simply means the choice of a building by the community for its use. In effect, this is a theology of dedication rather than consecration, since no holiness inheres in a place as such; if the community moves on, holiness moves on with it.

4.78   Parallels may be found in other faith traditions where the place of worship is essentially conceived as a place of the community's meeting. In Judaism, for example, the synagogue – literally the place of 'gathering together' – replaced the cultic centre of the Temple situated in the holy city of Sion; in Islam, the mosque is the 'place of prostration', defined by the Muslims meeting there to worship in the appointedway. Perhaps the clearest vision of holy place as the place of meeting and hospitality is provided by the *gurdwara*, where the Sikh community both gathers together and offers freely to all comers the shared meal of the *langar*. Sikhism has also, however, developed a tradition of shrine and pilgrimage which moves beyond this. The sense of some places as being special in so far, and only in so far, as special people meet there, is also of course found much more widely in society at large in the emphasis on the family home as a special place. The strength particularly of British home-owners' attachment to their dwelling places notoriously goes beyond purely financial considerations.

4.79   The church viewed just as meeting place raises no particular theo-logical or practical problems in dealing with the question of *disposal* of its buildings to other faith communities. When the community of faith no longer has need of the property, it is at liberty – on this understanding – to sell it to anybody. To pursue the parallel with homes, not many Christians, whatever their theological persuasion, would hesitate to sell their own homes to people of another faith, even though the purchasers might offer prayer in the buildings.

4.80   Questions of possible *use* of continuing church buildings by people of other faiths would seem to depend on the degree of security enjoyed by the Christian community, since this will govern the extent to which they can open up their home in hospitality to others. It is clear that there will be some boundaries here, both behavioural and geographical – there may well be some things you would not approve of happening in your own home, and there may be others you would tolerate in your entrance hall but not in your kitchen. In the same way, the Christian community might happily allow people of other faiths to use the church hall for religious ceremonies, but not the church itself; or distinctions might be drawn between nave and sanctu-ary. At the same time as drawing lines to safeguard their own security, though, Christian hosts have a clear duty to show the gracious hospitality of God to all. The question which must be faced by each host community is, how far and to what extent hospitality to *people* of other faiths entails hospi-tality to the *practice* of other faiths.

Places of memory

4.81   The equation of church building with mere meeting place is attrac-tive in its simplicity and in offering flexibility to a mission-oriented church; but it scarcely accounts for the depth of spirituality associated with church buildings in the experience both of Christians and of others. Indeed, it could be argued that such a reductively functionalist view owes as much to west-ern secularism as to authentic Christian faith. Richard Hooker, in *The Laws of Ecclesiastical Polity* (chapter xxv), judiciously remarked that churches are not merely 'provided that the people might there assemble themselves in due and decent manner', but also have 'a majesty and holiness which act as a sensible help to stir up devotion'. For Catholic and Orthodox Christians the holiness experienced in the eucharistic assembly is in some sense prolonged by reservation of the sacrament, and to see a lamp by the tabernacle is to be aware of a sacred presence surviving in the place beyond the departure of the congregation; similarly, icons and images evoke a consciousness of the saints continuously offering their prayers united with the visible church. These symbols make present for worshippers the remembrance of holiness experienced in particular times and places. Such memories of holiness may – as with the eucharist – be of universal significance, or they may – as with local cults of the saints – have a particular local reference; in either case, they point to a deep 'sacramental' dimension in what makes places holy.

4.82   Not all early Christian places of worship were private houses in cities. In imperial Rome, for example, the tombs of martyrs – generally outside the city where Roman cemeteries were situated – were revered from early days, and Christians would gather there particularly on their 'heavenly birthdays', the anniversaries of their martyrdom. During the fourth century, the permanent construction of churches over these holy places began; naturally, the martyrs' relics occupied a central place in the completed building. From this there developed a second element in the consecration liturgy- the deposition of relics in the church. This came to be seen as highly desirable, particularly as the influence of Roman liturgy spread throughout the West. An early example is known from 386: when St Ambrose was attempting to consecrate a new church in Milan by simply celebrating the eucharist in it, the crowd interrupted him to insist that they wanted it doing 'properly, like in Rome', i.e. with relics. Ambrose accordingly set to work digging nearby, and soon found two bodies which he identified as the relics of SS Protasius and Gervasius, who were duly enshrined in the new basilica. The supply of martyrs was not inexhaustible, however, and there soon grew up the practices both of dividing bodies for distribution to several churches and of using so-called 'secondary relics' – cloths or other objects which had touched a saint's body. Something like the cult of secondary relics is attested in the New Testament (Acts 19. 12), where the sick are healed by 'handkerchiefs or aprons' which have touched Paul's body. The cult of the martyrs is not evident within the New Testament, though the experience of martyrdom is presumably alluded to in Revelation 11. 3f. ('the two witnesses'), and Acts 8. 2 is careful to record the burial of Stephen by 'devout men who made great lamentation over him'. The tombs of the prophets, however, were venerated in first-century Palestinian Judaism (Matthew 23. 29f.), and similar attitudes may well have ben carried over into the early Christian community. There is certainly early evidence of the preservation and veneration of St Peter's relics at Rome.

4.83   The holiness of certain places here arises from their identification with stories treasured in the collective memory of the Christian community: holy men and women had, by their life and death, charged specific places with the energy of God's grace at work in them. We should also remember the great upsurge of devotion directed from the fourth century on to the holy places in Palestine. Jerusalem above all was holy through its association with the supreme story of the community of faith. Through the liturgies of Holy Week, that story could be dramatically re-enacted in other places; and through the cult of the Holy Cross – fragments of which were distributed throughout Christendom – churches everywhere could become sacred sites participating in Jerusalem's supreme sense of holiness through memory. In the Christianisation of western Europe, as well as universal memories like those provided by the cult of the Holy Cross, or the relics of the apostles or secondary relics of the Virgin Mary, a major part was played by more localised memories of monastic and other saints, whose shrines frequently served as foci of evangelisation and of devotion; they also were believed to act as spiritual fortresses providing protection against external foes. Within the medieval church, there was therefore a more or less constant tension between holiness mediated in particular places by symbols of local memory and attempts to interpret holy places in terms of the universal memory of Christianity. The numerous apparitions and images of 'Our Lady of Walsingham' (or Egmanton, or Willesden) can perhaps be seen as mediating this tension.

4.84   In post-Reformation Anglicanism, the cult of relics has been at most marginal, though pilgrimage to the shrines of Walsingham and Glastonbury is still popular. But a strong sense of churches' memory–holiness lives on through their association with burials, particularly where the building is surrounded by a graveyard. This can be for some a place of individual memories, but it also is widely seen as a remembrance of the collective story of a community: 'Each in his narrow cell for everlaid/The rude forefathers of the hamlet sleep'. This sense of holiness is by no means limited to the worshipping Christian community or to the graveyard. Those with a more tenuous connection may also have a strong sense of the holiness of the church, through its historical associations, its art, or particularly through its connection with key events in their life story, whether baptism, wedding, or funeral. Legally this is expressed in the protection from unjustified disturbance afforded to the graveyard by the ceremony of consecration.

4.85   A secularised cult of secondary relics is thriving in contemporary society, as periodic auctions of 'celebrity memorabilia' testify, and this is often linked to popular pilgrimages to places associated with famous figures, from Stratford-upon-Avon to Graceland. In many other faith traditions too, there is recognition of the holiness of places hallowed by the memory of their sacred story: Vrindavan where Krishna sported with the *gopis*, Karbala where Hussain was martyred, Bodhgaya where the Buddha attained enlightenment, and others. In some cases the holy memory is focused on a primary or secondary relic – the tombs of the Sufi *pirs*, for example, or the Temple of the Six Banyan Trees in Canton which was built over a fragment of hair of the Sixth Zen Patriarch.

4.86   *Disposal* to another community of a place hallowed by its story requires the removal of the associations which evoke the community's memory. This is easy enough to achieve in the case of the translation of relics – when the monks of Lindisfarne, for example, were threatened with Viking raids, they set off wandering through Northumbria with the bones of Cuthbert, until eventually they established a new centre of holiness at Durham as his resting place. It is more difficult in the case of a graveyard focusing a whole community's story; but even here there may come a time when the story no longer resonates with people, or the community itself has effectively died. Whether a graveyard is involved or not, the community may still focus its collective memories on the church, and then disposal – like closure – will be a controversial and probably unpopular step to take.

4.87   *Joint use* by faith communities of such places of holy memory can arise on the basis of a shared story, for example, the cave near Ephesus, by tradition a home of the Virgin Mary, which is visited by Christian and Muslim pilgrims alike, or the image of the Black Madonna of Siparia in Trinidad, venerated by Christians on the Second Sunday after Easter and by Hindus on Holy Thursday. More commonly, though, a holy place will hold different memories for different communities, and the challenge of shared use could only be met if each community's contemporary retelling of its own story can in some way make space for the other's memories. Around some holy spots, widely differing stories and memories cluster because people appear to sense something mysteriously numinous in the place itself.

Places of mystery

4.88 Alongside the eucharist and the deposition of relics, a third important element in consecration liturgy, especially the Gallican rites, is the use of various ablution and purification ceremonies. The underlying structure of the liturgy is parallel to that of initiation – the church is first symbolically baptised through sprinkling the altar and walls with holy water, then chrismated through the anointing of the same parts of the building. These rites reflect the tendency in the evangelisation of Europe for Christian missions to take over and 'baptise' places of pagan worship for use as churches. This policy was recommended to Augustine of Canterbury by Pope Gregory, who seems to have assumed that the situation in England was similar to that in Rome. With his Roman sense of the *genius loci*, he reasoned that by this means the English would 'be able to banish error from their hearts and be more ready to come to the places they are familiar with, but now recognising and worshipping the true God' (Bede, 1969, 1.30). Where communities did worship in such newly converted churches, there was surely a deep sense of continuity in maintaining recognition of the holiness once experienced in the ancient sanctuary. Mythically, this might be expressed through reinterpreting in a new context the old traditions of the place – so, for example, the Celtic legend of Glastonbury Tor as the place of burial of a magic cauldron of plenty is transmuted into the story of Joseph of Arimathea's burial of the Holy Grail. Liturgically, the baptismal ablutions, recognising a numinous power associated with the place, are designed to ensure that that power will be channelled through the wholesome mysteries of Christian faith. Nor has this sense of the power of a *mysterium tremendum et fascinans* (Rudolf Otto) identified with certain sites wholly lost its power even in modern Western Christianity; indeed, some contemporary charismatic thought and practice are insistent on the existence of local and territorial spirits, which may be far from benign.

4.89 A sense of the numinous attached to specific places – springs, wells, trees, groves, rocks, mountains – is in any case widespread in human societies. It may be becoming increasingly attenuated in contemporary urbanised Britain, though the popularity of mountain-climbing and hill-walking testify to a continued awareness of the significance of landscape. In relation to buildings, though, the sense of 'special atmosphere' is still strong even in secular terms, as is evidenced by the influence of the heritage lobby. Some other traditions of faith have been much less inhibited than Western Christianity in recognising and celebrating holiness inherent in certain places. In Japanese Shinto, for example, sacred trees and rocks are marked off by strings of folded white paper; these are designed to draw the passer-by's attention to the spiritual power *(kami)* resident in the place, and invite him or her to adopt an attitude of reverence. Similar demarcations of places invested with a distinctive sanctity are found in cultures around the world.

4.90   In cases of the *disposal* of churches to other faith communities, the new user of the building may well affirm the holiness of the place through its previous use as a 'house of God', and stress the continuity between present and past. This was, for example, the attitude of the Buddhists who purchased Holy Island in Scotland, or those who converted a Congregational church in Leicester into a Jain Temple.

4.91   Potent clashes over the *use* of places whose holiness is widely recog-nised can arise when rival faith traditions try exclusively to appropriate the site for their own use, refusing to make space for others' interpretations. The Indian Christian artist Jyoti Sahi likens this to 'two sons claiming a common inheritance, or struggling like twin brothers in the same mother's womb – the holy place is the womb which brothers tend to claim as their own inher-itance' (Sahi, 1993). But he also has a vision of places serving to unite people of different faith traditions – 'groups of believers can share a common sense of belonging to a holy place, without fighting over it'. He suggests that what needs to be envisaged is some way in which different faiths can provide dif-ferent but compatible means of access through which their faithful can be nourished by the holiness of a place and so also by the holy God who makes himself known there but is limited to no place. The situation in England is different in many respects; not all would share Jyoti Sahi's vision, though interesting experiments in shared holy places are being made in some chapels or 'religious spaces' in hospitals and other institutions.

Maintaining the linkages

4.92   Christian faith, in common with universal religious consciousness, thus recognises the holiness of God being mediated to us through particular places in different ways: through the gathering of his holy people there; through the rooting there of memories disclosing his holiness; through awareness of the mystery of his holy presence apprehended there. Contemporary Christians, especially in dialogue with people of other living faiths, need to recover an awareness of the richness and depth of the ways in which consecrated places and buildings are sacramental of the presence of the holy God; and it is only from such an awareness that we can adequately and responsibly address questions of churches' disposal to and use by those faith groups.

4.93   It is characteristic of biblical faith that the linkage and relationship between the holy people and holy places are expressed in different ways. In the Old Testament, 'nomadic' and 'sacral' traditions are interfused; in the New Testament, the Letter to the Hebrews complements its vision of the pilgrim people of God with an elaborate analysis of the imagery of the earthly and the heavenly sanctuaries. Similarly, as we saw in chapter 3, biblical awareness of the consecrated holiness of particular places is held in tension with recognition of the whole cosmos as less than the dwelling-place of God: 'But will God dwell indeed with men and women on the earth? Behold, heaven and the highest heaven cannot contain thee; how much less this house which I have built!' exclaimed Solomon, consecrating the temple in Jerusalem (2 Chronicles 6. 18). Other faith traditions also use different ways to link what points to the divine in one place to the universally holy. For example, in Islam, the whole world can be seen as a mosque pointing the Muslim to the worship of the transcendent God. For Hindus, the entire earth is Prithvi, the sacred mother from whose womb all life-forms are born.

4.94   Recognition of these linkages must provide the ultimate theological perspective to which all discussion of the shared use of consecrated buildings can be referred: people of all faiths share in our one earth, one holy place, though practising in it very different ways of life and interpreting it by very different stories and memories. It is clearly essential for us all to work out a pattern of shared use of this one cosmic sanctuary. Any progress at the local level in finding realistic and creative ways of sharing our holyplaces can be seen as ways of reflecting that universal sharing.

5

Disposal
Other Faith communities
and Anglican buildings

5.95   Even when the whole earth is seen as holy, people of most religious faiths want to have a place of their own where they can worship, teach the faith, and meet for fellowship. The faith communities of Britain are no exception. Christian communities may sometimes take their places of worship and community for granted, but members of other faiths, like many inner city parish churches, are often insecure minority groups. For them buildings are of central importance in bringing people together in worship, friendship and mutual support. Many of the buildings briefly described below will include facilities for education and social activities. The list makes no attempt to be exhaustive, but may throw some light on what people of other faiths look for in a building which is to house the week-by-week and day-by-day expression of their religious life.

5.96   The main place of **Jewish** communal worship and life in Britain is the synagogue, to which members of the Orthodox community walk. The synagogue includes a variety of symbols and objects relating to worship and community life, including the Ark of the Covenant containing the scrolls of the *Torah*, or first five books of the Bible.

5.97   The mosque is the **Muslim** place of prayer and the centre of community. It is known in Arabic as the *masjid*, the place of prostration. In it there is no furniture, but simply a carpeted floor, where those who pray stand united in humility and equality, for there must be nothing which would detract from the worship of God. Muslims pray facing Makkah (Mecca), the direction being marked in the mosque by a niche, the *mihrab*. The community gathers together in the mosque particularly on Fridays for the midday prayer.

5.98   The *gurdwara* (meaning 'the door of the Guru') is the **Sikh** place of worship and community. Sikhs believe that the holy book, the *Guru Granth*

Sahib, is their Guru, and the book is therefore central to worship and the only object which is venerated in the brightly decorated *gurdwara*. It is normally placed on a dais under a canopy and any member of the congregation may read from it during the services. The *langar* or kitchen is an essential part of the *gurdwara* and meals are served to all visitors as well as to the worshipping congregation. Hospitality is understood as worship and as service.

5.99   **Hindus** in Britain have, over the last twenty-five years, developed their temples or *mandirs* ('dwelling-places' i.e. of the divine) from a variety of buildings, including private houses. They also have a few diligently and skilfully designed purpose-built centres. In Britain they normally gather on a community basis and the temple will include facilities for education and social occasions. There is usually a hall which houses a main shrine and lesser shrines. The images are made of wood or marble, and are beautifully dressed and cared for. Various offerings, including flowers, are made during worship.

5.100   A range of **Buddhist** community, teaching and meditation centres of different traditions now exists in Britain, from very simple shrines and pagodas to large monastic complexes. A Buddhist building normally includes an image of one or more of the Buddhas ('enlightened ones').

5.101   It is easy for Christians to visit the places of worship and community of their neighbours of other faiths. Several organisations are willing to make introductions and to arrange meetings. Practical guidelines for understanding and visiting places of worship are included in *'Multi-Faith Worship'?* published by Church House Publishing for the General Synod Board of Mission in 1992.

5.102   A faith community new to a city or town will normally feel vulnerable and may therefore seek to share an existing centre for worship and community life as the only way forward in the first instance. Experience shows, however, that as soon as the opportunity occurs, the faith community will strive to move to premises where it has the sole use, or where it has total control. When seeking a building in which to worship, a redundant church or church hall is an obvious starting point, especially as a church will not require planning permission for a change of use. As the community establishes itself and grows in confidence and wealth, purpose-built temples, mosques, and *gurdwaras* are often created, sometimes by demolishing the redundant Christian building previously used and rebuilding on the site.

5.103   Disappointment and misunderstandings can occur when a faith community approaches Church of England diocesan authorities seeking to purchase or lease church premises for two basic reasons:

1. There is a lack of understanding of the constraints upon the use of Church of England redundant churches as distinct from those of other denominations.

2. The cost of maintaining a listed building, when purchased or leased, is under-estimated.

Lack of understanding of constraints

5.104   When a Muslim, Hindu or Sikh group sees a church or hall under-used or facing closure and is seeking worshipping premises and has funds available, it is often surprised by the difficulties which Church of England authorities raise. Generally there is no great difficulty in selling or leasing a church hall or other unconsecrated church property to another faith community for either community or worship use provided the incumbent and PCC (usually the managing trustees) agree and the diocese (usually the custodian trustees) has no objection. The Charities Act 1993 may require the sale or lease to be on the best terms which can be reasonably obtained, and publicity of the disposal to ensure this, but around the country there have been many examples of Anglican church halls being sold and developed in this way.

5.105   In general, the situation with regard to church buildings of Christian denominations other than the Church of England is the same as church halls. There are many examples of Methodist, URC and other redundant churches becoming temples, *gurdwaras* or mosques. When a Church of England church is facing redundancy, another faith community seeking new premises naturally supposes that negotiations can proceed as for a church hall or the church of another denomination. It is not easy to explain the complexities and difficulties of disposing of a redundant church in this way. Under the provisions of the 1983 Pastoral Measure, where a church is proposed to be (a) declared redundant OR (b) declared redundant and appropriated to another use, the diocese produces draft proposals which are issued to interested parties; when signed by the bishop these become the proposals from which the Church Commissioners produce the draft Pastoral Scheme. A church can be made redundant by a Pastoral Scheme under Section 28, the use being determined by a Redundancy Scheme under Section 51 (where slightly different procedures apply), or both procedures can be done together by a Pastoral Scheme under Section 46 or Section 47. This scheme is then tested by the Church Commissioners who are required to consult all interested parties. A new use for a redundant church can raise strong views which have to be properly considered. Use by another faith community could give rise to objections, particularly if non-Christian worship is involved.

5.106   The very comprehensiveness of the Church of England makes for vigorous debate and disagreement on some fundamental issues including the question of relations with people of other faiths. There will be members of the Church of England in any town or city who would wish to help those of other faiths to establish a community, teaching, and worship centre. Because they understand Hindus, Muslims and others as spiritual allies in a world mostly indifferent to the claims of God, they see nothing wrong in redundant church buildings being made available to become temples or mosques. Other members of the Church of England understand the uniqueness of Christ and Christian faith in the providence of God differently. For them this would exclude the use of a church, devoted to the worship of God through Jesus Christ, for any other purpose, and in particular for worship in or through any other name.

5.107   Because of this basic division a diocese would be unlikely to test a draft redundancy proposal involving the use of a redundant church by another faith community with the Church Commissioners until it had the agreement at least of the local incumbent, PCC and the Diocesan Synod. Even if this support was available it is likely that the matter would also need to be tested theologically.

5.108   Explaining this to Muslim or Hindu local leaders, anxious to find premises for a mosque or temple, is a sensitive matter but it can be done. Such people of faith do understand the issues surrounding a holy building. It has been known recently in England for a Hindu temple management body to be overthrown and replaced because it planned to extend the temple and in doing so to move the images. 'The images would not wish to be disturbed' was the opposition's reasoning. Similar feelings are engendered by the possibility of a change in a consecrated building, though for different reasons.

5.109   Secular planning and listed building control both apply to redundant churches and will limit what alterations are permissible to both exterior and interior.

The cost of maintenance

5.110 Assuming that the social and theological difficulties can be overcome, or even where the planned use of the redundant church does not include worship, there are still major financial difficulties. The reason that a diocese is prepared to declare a church redundant is usually because its maintenance has become too much of a financial burden for the modestly sized congregation. The building is likely to be listed and therefore needs to be maintained to the highest building standards – this can be extremely costly, though grants may be available. Hiring scaffolding to keep the public safe from decaying stonework, and repairing a roof using material specified by the local authority planners can cost very large sums of money.

5.111 The major cost to another faith community of taking on a redundant church is not likely to be that of purchase. In fact the church is often disposed of on the basis of a lease which requires the users to pay for all necessary repairs. It is the maintenance costs which can be grossly under-estimated. Most diocesan authorities have a catalogue of abortive negotiations with housing associations, other denominations and other non-controversial users, where schemes which seemed to be desirable, involving users who thought that they had adequate funds, have run aground when the true costs of maintenance became apparent.

5.112 It requires great sensitivity and patience to explain these financial realities to a member of another faith interested in leasing or buying a redundant church. The difficulties can so easily seem to be raised merely to prevent a church becoming a temple or mosque and the suspicion may be that the real reason for the objection may be theological, social or even racial. Diocesan authorities need to be open and honest about the range of difficulties at a very early stage so that faith communities do not invest hope and finance in schemes which are hopelessly unviable.

6

Use

The experience of hospitality

What can be learnt from church-to-church host/guest relationships?

6.113   Churches in England have gained considerable experience in recent years of sharing the use of their buildings with other Christian churches, and it is important to take note of this experience in formulating guidelines for comparable relationships with other faith communities. Differing cultural expectations may account in part for problems in both kinds of relationship, but there are of course significant differences in the two situations. Other Christian churches share with Anglicans a common faith and a common baptism in the name of the Trinity. Christian ecumenical relations have been developed over many decades, and have been undergirded by immensely detailed theological work. This has given a proper confidence to local Christians planning a variety of covenants and agreements to work and worship together. Christian relations with other faith communities by contrast are at present limited, fragile and often controversial.

6.114   Nevertheless, in compiling our own report we have found great value in the publication entitled *The Report of a Working Party on the Sharing and Sale of Church Buildings*, which was written for Churches Together in England (1993). It concerns relations between churches, and contains many important recommendations and guidelines which apply to the sharing of church buildings with those of other faiths as well as with other Christians. We quote below those which we think to be relevant to the situations envisaged in our own report. (It is important to remember that this report is addressed and refers to all churches in England, not only the Church of England.)

6.115   Noting that in parts of London and some other large cities there is much under-used church property the report recommends that there should be a central clearing house in London and other major centres. The function of such an office would be:

1. To maintain lists of those local churches willing to share their buildings (and those churches seeking accommodation).

2. To offer help and guidance to potential host (and guest) churches or to be able to point enquirers to someone who can shed light on their problem. For example, information about the availability of grants for the repair of church buildings; legal advice about the upkeep of listed buildings.

6.116   The report provides a frank and detailed set of guidelines, divided into points for guest, and points for host churches to bear in mind.

Guidelines for guest churches

Sharing a building (church or hall)

Where two or more churches share the same building there is an ecumenical relationship (even if it's a bad one!).

A sharing relationship should not be a landlord/tenant relationship nor should a guest church allow itself to be treated like other church hall users (e.g. the badminton club or the pre-school play group.)

This seems to imply a rather cavalier attitude to these 'outside' organisations which is at variance with the thinking of the 1972 report (see section 2.19).

As early as possible in the negotiating process the meetings should involve responsible lay members of both host and guest churches.

6.117   Some points obviously relate to cultural expectations which have caused problems in the host/guest relationship:

Times. Be realistic about how long your services take especially if there is more than one guest church. Allow time for preparation and clearing up afterwards.

Use of amplified equipment. The noise level of electrically amplified equipment should be monitored to avoid unnecessary disturbance to local residents.

Cleanliness and order. Discuss and agree arrangements. Who is to be responsible for what? Be sensitive to each others' needs. Is adequate storage available? If not , can it be arranged or can you manage without it?

Finance. While wanting to avoid a landlord/tenant relationship, buildings, nevertheless, cost money to run. They have to be heated, lit, insured, repaired and maintained. Sometimes even the hosts don't know what it costs per hour to run their hall or church. It is important to find out.

Access and closure arrangements. Unless there are legal restrictions you should be given a set of keys. Sometimes, however, this is not possible. Caretakers need to be involved in the spirit of any agreements. Parking facilities should also be discussed.

Troubleshooting. Don't wait for the first problem to arise. Set up a system with your hosts to deal with conflicts like allegations of abuse of the premises, not keeping to agreed times, feelings of resentment about your treatment, racism, etc.

Guidelines for host churches

6.118   Guidelines for the host churches are equally direct and practical.

All relationships with another church (even bad ones) are ecumenical.

A request from another church for the hire of rooms on a regular basis should not be dealt with by the hall booking secretary or caretaker.

The leadership of your church should be involved in any negotiations about a sharing arrangement at the earliest possible stage.

During the negotiating process it is important that all necessary information is given regarding finance, cost to the guest church, how maintenance costs are worked out, access to the building, storage, insurance and display of information. Areas which are not accessible should be stated clearly and procedures for dealing with complaints or problems should be outlined. Where there are no existing procedures these should be discussed and agreed.

Language can create great difficulty. A willingness to listen, patience and understanding, are asked for as you may be talking with someone whose first language is not English.

The church council or church meeting should always be involved in the final decision about a sharing arrangement and, if possible, should have the chance to meet representatives of the guest church beforehand.

Some form of written agreement is always highly desirable. The agreement should include provision of regular meetings between host and guest churches to review the relationship and iron out any difficulties.

If an enquiry for the use of the Church building or for a decision to have a formal sharing agreement is refused do not be mysterious about it. Give the real reason for refusal.

Where there is a signboard some space should be allocated to the guest Church for displaying their information, thus informing the community of their presence.

Seriously consider refusing any request to share from a church which is going to act in competition with you.

If in doubt about racist attitudes (yours or the other church's!) consult race relations advisers.

Members of the guest Churches are generally from different ethnic backgrounds, church traditions and customs. Openness and sincerity are a Christian way of dealing with fellow Christians. Where there are doubts or hurts dialogue is essential.

Communication is vital and the guest churches should be kept informed through regular meetings about general repairs and refurbishing as well as general activities. It is expected that this will be a two-way process.

Some useful points to remember

6.119   The pamphlet ends with detailed references to some of the issues which have caused most ill-feeling on the part of guest churches.

Payment by the hour per room is most dreadful and kills off all ecumenical spirit.

Do not leave your sharers in the cold. They also need warmth just as the host congregation does.

It is very inconvenient to lock up toilets when people are using the building.

Locking one end of the church is a fire hazard and is dangerous. If there are facilities you do not want your guest church to use, for a genuine reason, tell them about it. Do not suddenly hide things away.

Ministers must avoid hostility towards the guest church's congregation and children. Children are children and need the use of the recreational facilities on the premises.

Abusive language must not be used against anybody. Derogatory remarks and insults must be avoided.

Unnecessary fault finding and unbelievable excuses lead to a bad relationship.

6.120   Some of these last points in particular may seem to be unnecessary reminders of basic hospitality, but the working party concludes by noting that they come out of the 'sad and painful experiences' of guest churches. If such things need to be said to Christians sharing their buildings with fellow-Christians, it is, unfortunately, probable that they will be needed all the more in the context of inter-faith relations.

The practice of other churches

6.121   As yet, however, there is insufficient gathering of experience with communities of another faith in the role of guests for us to be able to put together guidelines of comparable detail. Even when we turn to our ecumenical partners there is not a lot to help us. Correspondence with other churches, both in Britain and abroad, suggests that either the situation has rarely arisen in their experience, or that no consistent practice has evolved and no policy been formulated. The concerns of the early 1970s (see chapter 2) seem to have been forgotten.

6.122   One exception to this general pattern is the **Religious Society of Friends,** whose London Yearly Meeting in 1994 approved a section of its *Book of Discipline* which reads:

> Other communities of faith often find our meeting houses acceptable venues for their own worship and meetings are encouraged to find out whether their premises could be so used . . . Meeting houses may also be used for multi-faith worship. The hospitality of worship which Friends can offer through silence may serve as a meeting point for many religious traditions.

6.123   A more conventional ecclesiastical attitude is exemplified by **Roman Catholic** authorities, who advise distinguishing between the use of actual church buildings by other faith communities, which is discouraged, and the temporary use of hall or classroom belonging to the church, which can be offered. The decision should be fully explained to parishioners.

6.124   The **British Methodist Conference** debated the issue of the use of Methodist church buildings by other faith communities in 1994, and decided to ask its Faith and Order Committee to produce a theological judgement on the appropriateness of allowing this, with the help of the Methodist Committee for Relations with People of Other Faiths. This move is intended to resolve uncertainty about the correct interpretation of the 1974 Methodist Church Act.

6.125   These decisions and debates, like the rest of this chapter, have been concerned with the *use* of church buildings by others. As noted in chapter 5, the Church of England follows different procedures from those of other churches in its *disposal* of church property. Like the General Synod of the Church of England, the **General Assembly of the Church of Scotland** has debated the question of the disposal of redundant churches. The common restrictions imposed by the General Trustees on churches and halls prohibit the use of such buildings or any future buildings erected on the same site for 'betting, gambling or gaming, for the sale . . . of alcoholic liquor or, unless specifically authorised by the Superiors, as a meeting house, meeting place or institution for any religious denomination or for religious purposes'. Some or all of these restrictions may be dispensed with at the request of local church bodies, and it is recognised that the religious restriction was included to prevent the sale of churches to the more extreme Christian groups whose views would be regarded as offensive by those who formerly worshipped in the building.

Conclusion

6.126   It is clear from the experience of hospitality offered by churches, even in relation to fellow-Christians, that there is real scope for misunderstanding and hard feelings unless great care is taken with the arrangements. It is highly desirable to develop a genuine relationship between the two (or more) communities of faith involved, and to ensure that the bond is not simply one of finance and convenience. At the same time experience suggests that this is not easy. Cultural and perhaps language barriers deter many from the attempt to make friendships across them. A church which decides to offer its premises for use by a community of another faith needs to weigh carefully what it has to offer apart from a sheltering roof. It may be wise to search among its number for some with a gift and a vocation for adventurous friendships.

7

The legal situation
and recommendations
on leasing and disposal

7.127   As we have been working on the subject of this document we have become aware of how deeply attached people become to the buildings which enable them to come together as worshippers, the bricks and mortar which help them to sustain and develop their religious life. This is likely to be true for any faith community, but will perhaps be particularly so in the case of churches which have stood for generations as landmarks and symbols of Christian faith. We have seen some of the reasons for this, the holy history by which people have lived (sections 2.32, 4.83) and the sacramental intention which has set apart buildings 'for ever' for the worship of God in Christ (sections 2.25, 4.70, 4.74). Anxiety about what will take place in a redundant church is also a factor in the reluctance to dispose of a church building to a community of another faith. As yet there is no general agreement in the Church of England about the character of worship outside the Christian traditions, and there is no real way of determining what happens in a former church building once it has left church control.

7.128   Against this it can be urged that the dominant New Testament tradition is the holiness of people rather than the holiness of place (sections 3.64, 3.65). God cannot be confined to a building, and the behaviour of those who use holy places may even drive him away (section 3.60). This may explain a certain ambivalence in the Church of England about the theology of consecration (sections 2.22, 2.41, 4.72). Many want us to focus on the role of the local church community rather than the character of its property (section 2.36), and call for a theology of hospitality rather than 'impregnability' (section 2.28). Sadly it seems that such generous hospitality has not always been evident in the churches of England (sections 1.3, 1.5), and even the experience of sharing premises with Christians from other churches has often been unhappy (sections 6.119, 6.120).

7.129   If the arguments are so balanced, we should perhaps take seriously the requirement to hold each in tension with the other (section 4.93). If the Church is a worshipping community in mission, the ultimate consideration must be the effect of any proposed sale of church property to another faith community on the church's own life and mission. The Church must not enable attacks on its own Gospel (section 2.17). Many would rightly remind us of the potential impact of such sales on struggling Christian communities in other parts of the world (section 1.8), but there is also some experience internationally of holy places shared between faiths (section 4.87), and an argument, made by the Indian Christian Jyoti Sahi, for making space for other visions of the whole earth as a holy place (sections 4.91, 4.94). In some English inner cities the sale of an unwanted church building to those of another faith community could be a powerful statement of Christian opposition to racism and xenophobia, and church commitment to the disadvantaged (sections 1.3, 2.20).

7.130   A key condition must be that there is no other local worshipping Christian community ready and able to take on the often considerable burden of repair and maintenance of the property (sections 5.110, 5.111). It would be quite wrong to cut short the Christian history and character of a building by offering it to those of another faith when that story might be continued by Christians of another confessional tradition.

7.131   It is not easy to explain to potential purchasers or leaseholders, especially of another faith, why a particular unused church cannot simply be made available to them. The procedures are complex and time-consuming, and all the while the building itself is likely to be deteriorating and subject to vandalism. Particular efforts need to be made to help people understand the constraints on the Church of England (sections 5.103–5.112).

The legal situation

7.132   The Church Commissioners make the final decision under the Pastoral Measure 1983 as to whether a redundant Church of England church should be preserved by the Churches Conservation Trust, sold or leased for a suitable alternative use, or demolished. The diocese concerned has a duty to seek a suitable alternative use and normally has a maximum period of three years within which to come up with a proposal. The Commissioners will then normally test this in consultation with a wide variety of interested groups. The Commissioners' current guidelines state that 'use for worship by adherents of a non-Christian faith is not to be regarded as an evidently suitable use', but is not altogether excluded. If the diocesan uses committee and the bishop support such a proposal after wide consultation in the locality, the Commissioners would prepare and publish a draft scheme to put it into effect. Subject to consideration of any representations it could then go ahead.

Wide consultation is the keynote of this process, to ensure that all interested parties have a say in the process. This can be time-consuming, and while it is going on the diocese has the sometimes difficult task of keeping an empty and unused church reasonably maintained.

If the diocese fails to find a use which they regard as suitable the Commissioners have to consider the options of preservation or demolition. While demolition under the Pastoral Measure 1983 enjoys ecclesiastical exemption and does not therefore require secular consents, the Commissioners have agreed that if their proposal to demolish a listed church (or a church in a conservation area) proves controversial, the Secretary of State for the Environment may call a non-statutory inquiry, and they will follow his subsequent recommendation. The Department of the Environment has indicated that, in such circumstances, the Secretary of State would be unlikely to recommend demolition unless he was satisfied that no othercommunity use (including use by another faith) was available.

Principles for disposal

7.133   Since final decisions are in the hands of the Church Commissioners we would urge the following considerations upon them:

The process

1.   There should be widespread local consultation to estimate the likely outcome of the lease or sale of a redundant church building to a variety of religious and secular bodies with a number of uses in mind. The basic consideration should be the responsibility of the local church for promoting the mission of God.

2.   A decision of this sort should be taken bearing in mind the feelings of the total local community, the effect upon Christian relations with those of other faiths in this country, and the possible impact on churches overseas.

3.   Where a decision is made not to sell or lease a Church of England church building to another faith community which has asked for it, the reasons should be clearly, sensitively and publicly given.

Priorities

1.   Priority should be given to local Christian bodies within the ecumenical movement represented by Churches Together in England (CTE) and the Council of Churches for Britain and Ireland (CCBI), and to Christian bodies which though qualified to be members of CTE or CCBI are not members.

2.   The next priority should be given to educational or social welfare use which will have clear benefits to the whole local community, especially its deprived sections. It may be that those who deliver such benefits are members of another faith organisation. Whoever assumes responsibility for the building, it may be possible and desirable to reserve part of it as a place for Christian prayer.

3.   Disposal of a church building to a community of another faith for its regular life and worship will need wide consultation and agreement if it is to be generally acceptable. The architecture and symbolic meaning of some churches may make such disposal inappropriate, since their Christian character could only be removed by alterations which would be regarded as vandalism.

8

The legal situation
and recommendations on use

8.134   The first responsibility of a Christian congregation is what will promote the mission of the Church and the integrity of the Gospel of Christ. We
believe that the use of church property should be offered to the wider local
community in terms that are consistent with the Gospel. No church will
make that offer to any and every applicant, but we believe that there are circumstances in which the use of church property can be offered with
integrity to communities of other faith, as part of the wider local community.

8.135   We have seen that much dissatisfaction has been felt by other
Christian congregations sharing a building with a host church (sections
6.118, 6.119). If there is to be such sharing, this ecumenical Christian experience suggests that a genuine and sustained attempt at hospitality must be
made, in which at least some members of the church congregation make
serious efforts at personal friendships with the visitors (section 6.126). If this
can be achieved, the results for the mission of the church may well be more
effective than a refusal, however principled, to allow the other faith community use of the premises.

8.136   We believe it is not possible to prescribe in any detail what kind of
use of its property by the other faith community the local church should
allow. The church council must decide what form of hospitality will obscure
the authority of Christ and the Gospel, and what will promote it. The Church
should not make it difficult for people to pray, and to pray in their own way,
but ritual forms of worship may not be compatible with Christian belief.

8.137   Most other faith communities do not want to use the church itself,
or the worship area of a complex of church buildings, and it is normally
inappropriate for them to do so (sections 2.16, 6.123).

The legal situation

8.138   The use of church buildings belonging to the Church of England is governed by ecclesiastical law. A consecrated church building has normally been 'set apart from all profane or common uses' for worship according to the rites and ceremonies of the Church of England 'for ever'; it is subject to the jurisdiction of the ecclesiastical court of the bishop of the diocese, and cannot normally be used for other purposes unless authority for the use in question is obtained from the court (by grant of a faculty) or conferred by legislation. A building which is licensed for public worship (and often 'dedicated') but not consecrated is also subject to ecclesiastical law and (except in some cases) to the control of the ecclesiastical courts. It is normally held on the terms of a charitable trust deed or other legal instrument which lays down the purposes for which the building is to be used.

8.139   So far as worship is concerned, the Canons of the Church of England lay down what forms of worship are and are not authorised in churches of the Church of England. There is provision in the Canons for the use of churches for worship by certain other Christian churches, but not for such use by other faith communities. The Church of England minister has discretion in certain circumstances to use forms of service which have not been specifically authorised by, for example, the General Synod, the Archbishops or the bishop of the diocese, but under paragraph 3 of Canon B5 these must be 'neither contrary to, nor indicative of any departure from the doctrine of the Church of England in any essential matter'.

As regards uses other than worship, Canon F15 prohibits a church from being 'profaned by any meeting therein for temporal objects inconsistent with the sanctity of the place' and Canon F16 provides that when a church is to be used for a play, concert or exhibition of films or pictures, the minister 'shall take care that the words, music and pictures are such as befit the House of God, are consonant with sound doctrine, and make for the edifying of the people'. The same principles would seem to be applicable to the use of the church for teaching or instruction of any kind.

8.140   As a result, it will not normally be legally permissible for a church building of the Church of England to be used for worship or teaching by another faith community. There are also major restrictions on the use of such buildings by other faith communities for purely social purposes, and in some cases use for those purposes will require a faculty from the ecclesiastical court, which may well be refused.

8.141   A church hall will normally be held on charitable trusts, or on the terms of some other legal instrument, which prescribe the purposes for which the hall may be used. Even where social activities by other faith communities can be brought within the terms of the instrument, they may well preclude the use of the property for non-Christian worship or instruction. However, it will be necessary to look at each case individually in the light of the legal documents and the nature of the proposed use. This will normally also apply in the case of a multi-purpose building intended for both worship and other activities and, depending on the circumstances, other restrictions mentioned above may well apply to at least part of the building.

Principles of use

8.142   Where parish churches are approached by another faith community asking to use their premises, we recommend that:

1.   Thorough discussion of the issue should take place in the Parochial Church Council, and wide agreement be secured so that the visitors can be made genuinely welcome.

2.   In every case the diocesan registrar should be consulted about the legal position.

3.   Such activities should normally be restricted to the church hall or ancillary areas distinct from the area used for Christian worship.

4.   In cases where a multi-purpose building is used for Christian worship and for other activities, and where the sanctuary can be screened off, this should be done and the sanctuary remain unused except for Christian worship. Christian symbols, pictures etc. should otherwise remain in place and undisturbed.

5.   It is highly desirable that some regular contact takes place between members of the Christian congregation and the other faith users of the church building. Regular meeting could involve occasions of inter-faith dialogue or the exchange of simple hospitality at the time of festivals. The expectation of regular meeting and building friendships should be explained to the other faith users at the time of the original agreement so that the arrangement is not regarded by either group as a merely commercial one.

6.   It is important to ensure that the church premises will at no time be used for teaching which constitutes an explicit attack on the Christian faith. The best way of achieving this aim is to develop the kind of relationships

mentioned above. Relationships built on mutual knowledge, trust and undertanding will provide a context in which agreed restrictions on the use of the church premises can be observed and enforced. It may be wise to check if the parent body of the group concerned is affiliated to the **Inter Faith Network for the United Kingdom**, an important organisation linking local and national faith communities. Its office is at 5–7 Tavistock Place, London WC1H 9SS (tel. 0171 388-0008).

7.   The arrangement needs to be monitored so that with changes of personnel the original principles of the arrangement remain in force.

8.   The same concern suggests the value of a written agreement, drawn up after consultation with the diocesan registrar. A written agreement may also contribute to the sharing of good practice on a wider scale.

Bibliography

Bede, Ecclesiastical History of the English Nation, Oxford, 1969.

The British Council of Churches, *The Use of Church Properties for Community Activities in Multi-Racial Areas* (Interim Report, 1972).

The British Council of Churches, *The Community Orientation of the Church* (Final Report ,1974).

The British Council of Churches, *The Use of Church Property in a Plural Society*, 1980.

Church House Publishing, *Faith in the City*, 1985.

Church House Publishing, *Towards a Theology for Inter-Faith Dialogue*, 2nd edn, 1986.

Church House Publishing, *'Multi-Faith Worship'?* (GS 1011), 1992.

Churches Together in England, *Report of a Working Party on the Sharing and Sale of Church Buildings*, 1993.

Cross, F.L., *Oxford Dictionary of the Christian Church*, 2nd edn, OUP, 1974.

Davies, J.G., *The Secular Use of Church Buildings*, SCM, 1968.

Eusebius of Caesarea, *Ecclesiastical History*, Penguin, 1975.

The General Synod of the Church of England, *The Use of Church Properties for Community Activities in Multi-Racial Areas: Memorandum of Comment*, Standing Committee of the General Synod (GS 135),1973.

Hatchett, M., *Commentary on the American Prayer Book*, Seabury, 1980.

Hick, J., *God and the Universe of Faiths*, Collins/Fount, 1977.

Holm, J. with J. Bowker (eds), *Sacred Place*, Pinter, 1994.

Holmes, A., *Church, Property and People*, British Council of Churches, 1973.

Hooker, R., *The Laws of Ecclesiastical Polity*, published from 1594.

Otto, R., *The Idea of the Holy*, 2nd edn, Oxford, 1950.

Religious Society of Friends, *Book of Discipline*, Yearly Meeting, 1995.

Sahi, J., 'Proposal for a Study of Sacred Places as Common Ground', privately published, 1993.

Turner H.W., *From Temple to Meeting House: The Phenomenology and Theology of Places of Worship*, The Hague: Mouton, 1979.

Willis, G.G., 'The Consecration of Churches down to the Ninth Century' in *Further Essays in Early Roman Liturgy*, SPCK, 1968.